A Touch of Class

For Australian Cake Decorating

A Touch of Class

For Australian Cake Decorating

By Gail Dorter

Photography by Stephanie Barnes

Production Co-ordination , Artwork & Design
Bruce Gordon
Perth, Western Australia

Typesetting by
Typestyle,
East Perth, Western Australia

Printed by
Lamb Print Pty. Ltd.
East Perth, Western Australia

Colour Separations by
Prepress Services, WA. Pty. Ltd.
Leederville, Western Australia

Photography by
Stephanie Barnes

Author
Gail Dorter
P.O. Box 79, Hillarys, Perth, Western Australia

National Library of Australia
ISBN 0 646 01274 6.

It is necessary in a book of this type to name all the flowers described within. Many are indeed life
like, while some bear only a passing resemblance to their namesakes. I hope 'Mother Nature' will
forgive me.

All the cakes, flowers & ornamental pieces described &/or pictured in this book are the work of the
Author Gail Dorter.

Contents

Glamorous cream Cattleya Orchids with golden centres are the primary features of this elegant oval wedding cake. Tiny white Double Blossom, plus ivy stems, and cream ribbon loops compliment them. Ribbon insertion, two gold rings, and filigree in graduated sizes round the base add extra elegance. The pillars measure 6" and 11" high, with serviette rings slipped on the top and bottom of each for added interest.

S ince the publication of her first book *"CUTTER CLASS Flowers for Australian Cake Decorating"*, in 1987, **Gail Dorter** has been kept busy designing new cakes as well as answering questions from cake decorators worldwide. It was these questions that prompted this second book.

A lifelong ambition to decorate cakes, a mother who was a florist, and a background in making artificial flowers has stood her in good stead. "Being introduced to *Sue Wells*, and joining the *Cake Decorators Association of Western Australia* was one of the best moves in my life" she says. "It fostered my competitive nature, helped me with decorating problems and provided friends with the same interests."

Gail leads a busy life, juggling her cake decorating and floristry business with the role of wife and mother. She is supported in this by her husband *Peter*, who as well as being chief board cutter and pillar maker, also helps with advice and encouragement. In their few moments of spare time they enjoy fishing from their boat, with son *Matthew*, and friends.

I n 1981 when I began cake decorating, cutters were just making an appearance. Although they were available, there were no instructions. In order to use them it was necessary to work out feasible methods for creating other than tiny little biscuits! Fortunately I had some previous background in artificial flowers, and so perhaps had a head start. In 1987 it culminated in the writing of my first book *CUTTER CLASS Flowers for Australian Cake Decorating.*

What I didn't realise, was the wealth of incidental information I had collected on the way to its publication. Although I thought everyone knew all these little hints and tips, it has become obvious from correspondence I have received that it is not the case.

Cake decorators are continually improving their methods, as am I. This new book is an attempt to share some of the good ideas I have been shown, or simply stumbled across, as well as introduce some pretty new flowers.

I hope it will help you in your creative efforts.

FLUTE - Rest the petals on your index finger. Hold the fluting tool between the thumb and first three fingers of the other hand, and with a "roll and press" action, work backwards and forwards around the petal. Practice will pay dividends!

MOVEMENT - To lift and slightly twist petals *(as opposed to frilling them)*. Rest the petal on your index finger. Hold the fluting tool between the thumb and first three fingers of the other hand, and roll it very firmly forwards around the petal.

FINGER EDGES - Use your thumb and fingers to gently smooth and flatten out rough edges, and where required, to rub chalk colouring into petals.

PAINT CALYX - Thin some royal icing with water, or melt moulding paste *(see page 11)*, and colour it. Use a brush, suitably sized for the flower under construction, to paint a calyx on to the back of the flower. This not only holds the flower firmly on its stem, but when fixed into sprays, that little extra bit of green adds a natural look to arrangements. Because the flowers are neatly and realistically finished, it is not necessary to hide the backs of them, so fewer flowers are needed.

CURL EDGES - Place the flower on soft foam, and using a ball tool, gently press and pull towards the centre of the flower. Curl each petal separately, and always start at the very edge, and stop before reaching the centre of the flower.

POLLEN - Pollen adds a softening look to icing flowers, and is easily made. Simply put fresh desiccated coconut through a blender, then sift out and keep the finest particles. One teaspoon of this is sufficient for dozens of small blossoms. It can be tinted to any colour using scraped chalks. One note of warning though - if you put the coconut through the blender too long, it will be reduced to an oily consistency - totally unsuitable. There are many other foodstuffs that can be used as pollen, but coconut is the only one that is white, and therefore can be tinted to any colour.

STAMENS - Both sizes of stamen are used, as well as the flat ones, depending on the size of the flower. If you are just beginning on cutter flowers, use the large ones until you become adept at pulling them through without the flower sliding down the stem. For small flowers I use mainly white stamens which I chalk or spray to suit my own colour schemes. The range of stamens has increased since my last book, and there are some extremely fine ones available now. It is worth hunting for them, as they are daintier in flowers that require a lot of stamens

WIRE - I use very thin non rusting florist wire *(26 gauge)*, and in most cases cover it with white or green florists tape before inserting it in the flowers. If you wish you can also substitute thin spaghetti on some flowers.

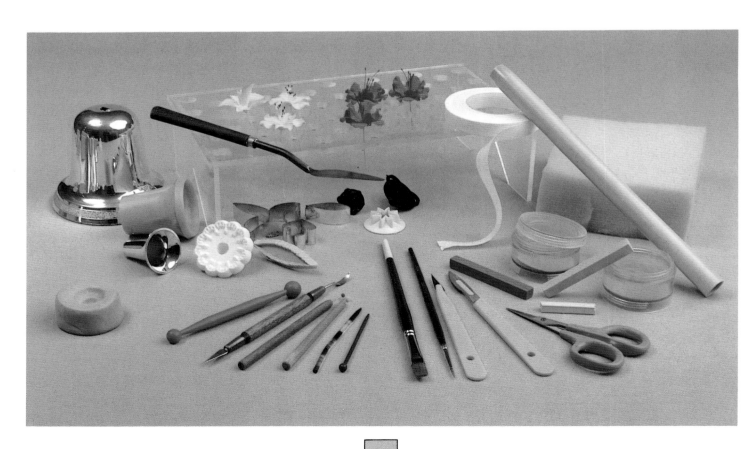

To successfully create flowers from cutters you will need a few basic tools.

A piece of **SOFT FOAM** which should be of fine consistency, and kept free of little grains of icing. **BALL TOOLS** of various sizes. I use such items as dressmakers pin heads, curler pins, swizzle sticks, and a melon baller - as well as commercially made ball tools.

You will also need a **FLUTING TOOL,** such as a short length of knitting needle, the end of a paint brush, or a curler pin for small flowers. A length of plastic piping makes an excellent **ROLLING PIN.** Something flat and smooth to roll the paste out on is a must. I have an acrylic board which was purchased as a "scrap" from a plastics retailer. Vinyl place mats are also excellent, especially if you have metal cutters that tend not to cut properly - the vinyl has some give, so the cutters generally work better. A good pair of long **TWEEZERS** are a must for inserting stamens, lifting flowers, and arranging them in sprays.

It is necessary to rest the flowers in or on something until they are dry. Small flowers with stamens as stems can be pushed into florists foam *(OASIS).* For larger flowers, you can utilise egg cartons, or cardboard fruit trays. Better still, try making a **HOLED BOARD.**

Holed boards are essential for cutter flowers, and handy for pulled ones. They allow flowers to dry while holding their shape, and are invaluable if you are transporting them any distance. They are neither diffucult nor expensive to make.

Many materials can be used. As long as it is approximately 5 or 6 millimetres *(1/4 inch)* thick, and able to be drilled, it is suitable.

Cut the board to the size you feel you need, mark where the holes are to be, and with a 6.35mm *(1/4inch)* bit, drill the initial holes. Use a counter sinking tool to round them out, and if necessary sandpaper any rough spots. Add legs, and it is ready for use.

My boards are acrylic, 15cm x 27cm long and 7cm high *(6in x 11in and 3in high).* For convenience I use a much smaller one for classes and demonstrations.

The idea of melting moulding paste came to me some years ago, when on the eve of a prestigious show I broke a petal off a vital flower in an arrangement. It had to be fixed quickly, and preferably invisibly. I knew it would be difficult matching the colour of the flower in royal icing, so decided to melt some left-over moulding paste. It worked beautifully, but it was so fiddly trying to melt a tiny bit of paste in a double boiler that the idea was shelved. However, since I have discovered the magic of microwaves, I have realised what a great idea it was.

The method is simple. Put a small amount of paste into a tiny container *(I use a plastic pill dispenser kept from a hospital stay),* add several drops of water, and zap for a few seconds. You need to watch and catch it before it boils, or you will have toffee. It must be stirred well, and then used fairly quickly before it sets. Sitting the container in hot water will help, and it can also be put back in the microwave once more, but again, don't let it boil.

As I stated previously, it is ideal for repair work, as it dries quickly and blends in perfectly. It is useful on flowers that are to be dipped, because not only is it less affected by the moisture than royal icing is, but being of the same medium as the basic flower, it accepts the colour to the same density.

Remember that melted moulding paste is stronger than royal icing, so keep it in mind for all the fiddly little things you do.

One more tip which you may find useful if you are using powder colours to tint some paste: Melt a small amount of your paste, *(minus the water)* then add the powder, and stir well. The heat from the paste will burst the little colour buds, and you will have maximum colouration, which means no horrible spotting or streaking. Keep stirring the paste till it cools, then work it into your moulding paste a little at a time, till the colour is right. You may have to let the finished paste rest a few minutes before you use it, but it is still far quicker than the conventional method.

If you wish to melt moulding paste without a microwave, then use the double boiler method, and add hot water to the paste. It will work in the same way, even if it takes longer to prepare

Moulds

Many flowers need to be made in a mould to help establish their shape. It is possible to buy some commercially made forms, but it is easy and inexpensive to make your own.

Firstly, transfer the patterns from below on to a piece of stiff cardboard, or soft plastic such as the lid of an icecream or margarine container. Cut them out.

Prepare some leftover moulding paste, or childrens putty *(purchased from a toy store)*, by pressing it into a small container, or simply make it into a block.

Gently form a hole in the centre *(a small ball tool is pretty handy)*, then use the pattern piece as a guide for the correct shape, turning it so the hole is even. The finished mould should correspond with the pattern. Round off the edges, and set aside to dry thoroughly. If you wish to preserve your mould it can be painted or sealed.

Use piping nozzles to start the holes for long thin shaped moulds, and if you need bigger flowers simply make bigger moulds. Wherever possible, use fresh flowers as a guide to making moulds.

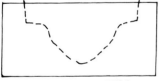

Hibiscus

Nerines

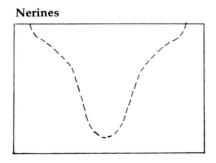

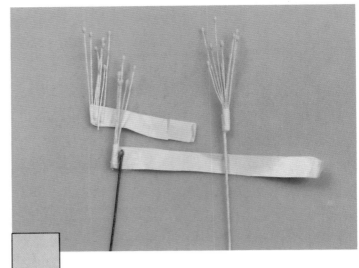

Stamens on Stems

All flowers are easier to arrange if they are on a stem, so incorporating the centre of the flower with a stem makes sense.

Cut the stamens to the required length, hold them in your right hand, with the stamens side by side, and the cut ends level. Rest a piece of florists tape across your left index finger, and lay the stamens over the tape, about 0.5cm *(1/4in)* from the end. Use your left thumb to fold the end of the tape over the stamens, then roll them up tightly. Once secure, insert a length of 26g wire next to the stamens and continue taping down the length of the wire. Don't simply "bandage" the wire. The correct way is to twist the wire with your left hand, while gently stretching the tape with your right hand. You may find it easier if you cut the tape to half its width.

Dried cornsilk makes very realistic stamens, provided you use silk that is nice and yellow, not withered and brown, or too green. Take several strands of silk about 2.5cms *(1in)* long, and bend a piece of wire across the centre, and down into a tight hook. Tape the stem, starting right at the top so the silk is held firmly in place. Trim the stamens, and with a brush dipped in very thin royal icing tip as many ends as possible.

For a rose centre, part the stamens in the middle, and flatten them evenly round the wire stem. Pipe a dot of royal icing in the centre, sprinkle on some pollen, and shake off any excess. Dip a paintbrush in caramel or light brown liquid food colouring, and gently tip the ends of the cornsilk.

If the silk becomes too dry and brittle to use, put it in a plastic bag, and spray a fine mist of warm water over it, then seal up the bag. It soom becomes pliant again, but don't leave it sealed in the plastic too long, or it reverts back to its original form.

Glass ornaments are often provided by brides for inclusion on their cakes. I usually try to keep it the main feature, and not allow the flowers and embroidery to become overpowering. On this simple cake I used apricot Iceberg Rosebuds, Eriostemon and sprays of cream Basic Blossom and buds. The cakes were 12", 10", 8", and 6", and the clear acrylic pillars were 3" high.

In order to give finished flowers and leaves a natural, slightly waxy look, they can be steamed. It is not a difficult process, but care must be exercised, or you can spoil flowers that may have taken hours to make.

There are really only two things to remember, the first is quite obvious - you will need stems on the flowers, or risk a burn to your fingers. The second thing you need to know is that steaming only works on flowers that have been made with a paste that incorporates Copha *(solidified oil)*. If you use a recipe that does not include Copha, a small amount can be added when you are working up your paste, prior to making the flowers.

Steaming will "set" the colours on chalked flowers beautifully. It will also enhance the finish on flowers that have been dipped. If you fancy leaves with a heavier shine, then steam them twice, allowing them to dry between treatments.

How do you actually do it? Easy! Simply pass your flowers, one at a time, through a head of steam, about 25cms *(10 ins)* away from the source, then stand them in florist foam to dry. Initially they will look just plain wet, but don't panic. Set them aside where they can dry fairly quickly, *(so they dont have time to sag)*, and the finished result should be a far more natural looking flower.

There is an alternative to steaming, that of lightly spraying the flowers with spray-on non-stick cooking oil. However, you run the risk of the spray spitting, and also the possibility of dust etc sticking to the finished flowers. It is not as good a method as the steaming.

Colouring and highlighting icing flowers with chalks is easy and effective. Almost any shade or tone can be attained simply by scraping the chalks with a sharp instrument, and mixing the resulting powders. To avoid streaking, it is generally best to mix the chalks with another white medium, such as potato flour *(cornflour can also be used, but it is not quite as effective as the potato flour)*.

On large flowers, chalking is done first, before any shaping and while the icing is soft. Dust on the powdered chalk with a soft brush, blow or brush off any excess, then blend it into the icing with your thumb. It is essential to do this first if petals are to overlap. Flowers done this way can be highlighted with extra colour once dried.

For dry flowers, use a soft, flat brush, dip it in the chalk, and drag the flat side of the brush across the edge of the petals. Some of the chalk will flick off onto the petals, but you will find the colour is concentrated on the edge, and fades in towards the centre. Shake off any excess. If you want intense colour on just the very edge, hold the flower upside down so the chalk can't fall back on the petals. You can add a deep red edge to rose leaves with this method.

It is not necessary to buy dozens of different chalks, as they are easily mixed and blended. With just a few basic colours you can create almost any hue. If you are stuck for a particular shade, then try dipping white chalk in liquid colour. Once it has dried it can be used in the normal way. To turn bright pink into a soft dusky colour, add a scrape of green. To take the harsh tone off yellow, add a little pink. A lot of colours can be deepened with a tiny bit of black. If you have difficulty matching up a fabric colour, try separating a few threads. Quite often the material will be made of two or three different coloured threads woven together, and you can use them as a guide to mixing a matching chalk. Just remember to always add potato flour, and only a little colour at a time when mixing new shades. For a perfect finish to your chalked flowers, "set" the colours by steaming them.

Colouring by Dipping

For years decorators have been painting and high-lighting flowers using a mix of food colouring and various alcohol based mixtures - Gin being one of the most popular agents.

The idea has been that the alcohol would dry or evaporate quickly, leaving the colour on the flower. Therefore it becomes obvious that the higher the alcoholic content of your mix, the quicker the flower will dry, and the better the results. Obviously pure alcohol is perfect, but unfortunately not always available. Here in Western Australia it is possible to buy natural cooking concentrate Vodka, which has an 80% alcohol volume. If you are unable to purchase a similar product, then check on some of the clear liqueurs available at your local liquor outlet. Polish Spirits is an excellent substitute, *(though more expensive)* and has the advantage of being drinkable should you fancy a tipple *(unlike the concentrate)*.

Even armed with this information, the results of painting colours on with a brush are not really that good. Kevin Work of Adelaide opened my eyes to the perfect solution. DIPPING!

The actual technique is simple - hold the flower by the stem, dip it in the prepared solution, then spin the flower to flick off the excess liquid, leaving nice even coloration. If you follow a few basic rules, you can colour flowers beautifully, and easily using Kevin's method.

Firstly, for really good results, you need to add some copha *(solidified oil)* to your paste *(some recipes include copha, in which case it is not necessary to add any extra)*. Simply take a small amount and work it into the paste. Rub a little into your hands, and on to the board before rolling out. This has a side benefit - if you do it regularly, it ofsets the drying effect that icing sugar and cornflour has on your hands.

Obviously you need something to hold on to, so a decent stem is a must.

Even though the alcohol solution dries very quickly, it still wets the flowers, so all petals must be securely attached. To this end, it is best to use thinned melted moulding paste *(see page 11)* where you would normally use royal icing, as it is less affected by moisture.

Have your mix in containers wide enough, and deep enough to accommodate the flowers you are dipping. Dip them in long enough to wet them, but not soak them till they start to sag.

Have a large empty container handy and twirl the flowers within it, unless of course you wish to redecorate your walls and furniture, not to mention yourself. A piece of foam in the bottom is advisable, as sooner or later you will drop a flower, and it may survive a soft landing.

If you want a white centre, or perhaps to keep the original colour on a central stamen *(as in violets)*, then paint the parts you don't wish coloured with melted copha before dipping.

If you want a rich deep colour, such as red, then add powder, rather than liquid to the alcohol.

Remember when mixing colours that they will tend to dry a little darker than they appear when wet. Save any broken or unsuitable flowers for testing colours on, and let one dry first, before going ahead and perhaps being sorry later.

If you want a highlight effect, such as a darker centre or tips, then you can chalk it on first, or paint it with a deeper alcohol mix before dipping.

Flowers that have pollen in them should be dipped before finishing off. Also remember that if you use coloured stamens they will be even darker once dipped, and may alter the overall colour of the finished flower.

If you are colouring really big flowers, then they can be quickly and liberally washed with solution using your biggest brush, then twirled as usual.

As the alcohol can be expensive, only mix small amounts at a time, and use containers with good seals for storage, to minimise evaporation.

With the dipping method you can make flowers in all the colours that have traditionally only been attainable with an airbrush. For reds, bergundys and other rich tones, make the flowers in lightly coloured paste first, then dip.

You will also find that dipped flowers have a different, slightly translucent look about them that is highly desirable. So buy yourself some alcohol, and start experimenting with all those old flowers you have made and never used.

Using a hinged cake leveller which wraps around odd shaped cakes. Simple right-angle levellers pictured to the side.

While it is essential that tiered cakes all be level, there is no doubting that levelling makes any cake easier to decorate. If your cakes are regularly the same height, embroidery patterns will always fit, and clients will always know how much cake to expect.

However, various factors, such as oven hot spots, and too firm or soft a mixture conspire to work against achieving perfect cakes every time.

There have been many methods to correct this over the years, but I believe I have the simplest method of all.

I use a piece of stainless steel, bent at right angles to form an "L" shape. I sit the cake in the crook of the "L", and slice off any excess with a long knife resting across the steel. Obviously the cake must be turned, but it is extremely quick and easy to do. I have five "levellers", all cut to different heights for tiered cakes. The levellers are available commercially here in West Australia, but if you are unable to purchase some, they can be home made using two pieces of wood or laminated chipboard, screwed or hinged together. To help you make your own, here are the dimensions of mine;

They are all 25cms *(10ins)* long on both sides. The heights start at 50mms *(2ins)* for top tiers, and go up in 7mm *(1/4in)* jumps. A standard three tier cake would be 50mm *(2ins)*, 57mm *(2-1/4ins)* and 65mm *(2-1/2ins)*. For a two tier cake, omit the central 50mm *(2-1/4ins)* tier.

The stands for this very elegant cake were fashioned to match the table centre pieces supplied at the function centre. The Cattleya Orchids are accompanied by Jasmin (with stamens) and lots of double Forget-me-nots. Graduated filigree lace pieces encircle the 12" 8" and 5" hexagonal cakes, and a matching keepsake bouquet balances the cake placements. The cake stands measure 7" and 14" high.

Cut a length of painted cardboard tube to required size. Sew a tube (or sock) of stretch fabric, and ease it on to the prepared tube.

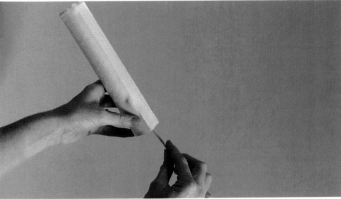

Use a knitting needle to straighten the seam, then fold the excess fabric at each end down into the tube.

Screw a solid wooden dowel (square or round) on to the covered presentation board from beneath (counter sink the screws). Drop the prepared pillar over the dowel.

Screw a flat disc of acrylic or painted chipboard into the support dowel, remembering to have the screws countersunk.

Pillars

There is nothing so sad looking as a wedding cake that has tilted due to lack of support. This usually occurs when a decorator assumes that cake pillars alone hold up multi tiered cakes. They don't! The pillars camouflage what DOES hold up a cake, which is usually a wooden skewer. On some cakes I have substituted clear acrylic rod for wooden skewers, but the principle always remains the same. If you don't have access to acrylic rod, then paint your skewers white, or cover them with silverpaper or alfoil if they will be showing. Once you have accepted that you must always use a firm support which goes through the cake and rests on the board beneath, then you can start creating pillar ideas of your own.

If you have pillar designing in mind, you will see potential everywhere you look. Cardboard rolls covered in fabric, stiffened and piped tulle, acrylic florists' cylinders or plastic containers covered in cotton lace, silver or crystal serviette rings *(lying flat)*, small vases (upturned over the skewers) are all possibilities. The range is even greater if you use objects which are strong enough to support the tiers themselves. However, in order not to have that sinking effect they must stand firmly ON skewers, not on the cake itself. With this in mind the list is only limited by your imagination. You can try crystal glasses, small vases *(standing upright)* strong serviette rings standing on edge, small ornaments, or classic silver salt and pepper shakers (lids removed). Clear and twisty acrylic pillars are also used in the same way, so for those who are new to cake decorating some instructions may be appreciated. Firstly, your cake needs to be as level as possible for them to look their best. Mark where they are to go, and push the skewers in, point first, keeping them straight not angled. Pull them out with a twisting motion, and re-insert them with the flat end first. Make sure they are resting on the board and not a nut which will shift later. Stand a pillar on the cake next to the skewer, and draw a pencil line level with the top of the pillar base on it. Remove the skewer, and cut it off at the pencil line, making it as straight as possible *(a mitre box is a great help)*. Re-insert the skewers in the cake, paint the top white, brush on some thin royal icing, and stand the pillars on them. Check that the pillars are resting on the skewers, and won't dig into the icing when you add the next tier. If you are satisfied, then rest the next tier on top, and gently push the pillars so that they are perfectly straight. Leave it this way until the royal icing has had time to set, and they will then be very safe and solid. You will find that the moisture from the royal icing will swell the skewers and they will be very firmly stuck to the pillars.

If your cake was not exactly level, you may have to add some height on one or more pillars to keep the next tier level -a small square made of dry moulding paste can be glued on if this becomes necessary.

Six Serviette rings make an unusual central pillar for this scalloped oval cake. (3 on the base, 2 in the centre and 1 on the top tier). As there is no actual weight on them, they are easily held in line with sticking tape. The sprays consist of Spray Carnations, Eriostemon and Basic Blossom. Silver ribbon above the lace and extension and 2 doves holding a trail of embroided flowers complete the decorations. See page 23 for how the pillars work.

Lace can be the perfect finishing touch on cakes, but the making and placing of it can be a major headache. The right tools, helpful hints, and fresh icing go a long way towards making it less of a chore.

Firstly, prepare the surface on which you will pipe your lace. Freezer paper is excellent, but even better is the clear wrap that florists use. When piping lace, hold the icing bag in your left hand, and write with the tube as you would a pen. It takes a while to get into the habit of squeezing with your left hand while writing with the right, but once mastered, will save you hours of tedious piping *(reverse instructions for left handers)*. A student with arthritis told me she found it easier to pipe lace pieces if she turned the pattern sheet on its side, so if you are having problems, try her idea.

Always use fresh icing, and don't add acetic acid, which will help it to dry quickly, but will also make it brittle. Never make lace too far in advance. As long as you can put it in a warm dry place, then two or three hours is time enough for it to dry sufficiently to handle. Old lace generally breaks far more often than freshly made pieces.

Use a curved handle pallette knife to lift the lace pieces off the paper. I regularly rub the blade of mine between a piece of folded sandpaper. Over the years it has become as thin and sharp as a razor blade, and slips easily under lace and filigree.

Tilt your cake to attach lace pieces, and the laws of gravity should ensure that they hang straight down. Once you right the cake, all the lace pieces will be evenly angled.

If you are using flooded lace pieces *(such as the leaves on page 47)*, don't flood them too heavily. Notice that the veins should still be visible. If you wish to cheat, you can buy small leaf, key and bell cutters, and cut them out of very thin moulding paste.

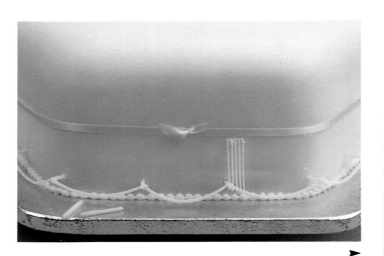

►

Don't be afraid to try filigree - the small pieces I have given the patterns for are easily handled. Ideally they should be piped with an "0" tube, and in the same way as you make lace. Always pipe a dot on the bottom left hand corner of each piece, to facilitate attaching it later.

I generally place my pieces at 1cm intervals, as it makes it easy to estimate how many pieces I need by just measuring round the cake.

Set your dividers at 1cm *(or whatever distance you have decided on)*, and step them off round the very base of the cake, leaving only tiny pinpricks. Pipe small snail trail round the cake, working it so that every fourth dot regularly covers a pinprick. *(only pipe a centimetre or so at a time)* Lift off a piece of filigree, and push it into place. The dot you piped on the corner of the filigree should go into the royal icing. In this way the lace pieces are held neatly, and almost invisibly, in place.

Remember when preparing and covering your cake that the sides must be smooth, as well as perpendicular, for the pieces of filigree to fit. It is also essential that you use a sturdy board, for if it flexes when you lift the cake, all the filigree will pop off.

Once you have mastered bridge and extension work, you may fancy a new challenge, and dropped loop extension is just that. Finished cakes have a lovely light airy look and will elicit much admiration and many compliments. It is not really difficult so much as requiring plenty of patience. I do not recommend it for damp or humid climates, so don't frustrate yourself by attempting it when you know the weather will defeat you before you start. As usual, by following a few basic rules, and applying some hints, the task will be easier.

Dropped loop extension is done on dropped loops, as the name implies, but not on rows of loops built out from the side of the cake as is usual. Instead, tiny "sticks" of previously formed and dried moulding paste are inserted in the cake at regular intervals, and dropped loops are piped off them. Never make the loops too wide, for the wider the loops the weaker they become. I generally use a No 1 nozzle for the loops, although you could well use a No.2 if they are fairly long ones.

Always tilt the cake up at the back when piping the connecting lines from the cake to the loops. This way they hang straight, and neither sag, nor put pressure on the loop base. Take care not to break the loops as you attach the down pieces. Each new addition will transfer more moisture to the loop, so you must work fairly quickly, as the longer you take, the more chance there is of breaking it. When you have to stop, try to do so at the top where one of the icing pegs is supporting the base loop. If you must stop half way across a loop, give that section time to dry before recommencing - I usually restart at the beginning of the next loop, and fill in later.

Because of the extreme care needed when attaching each down piece, the finish at the base will not be as neat as with conventional extension work, so pipe another dropped loop across the bottom to tidy it up and add strength at the same time.

Presenting Your Cake

When designing a cake, give some thought to the board on which you will present it. Size, shape, covering, and colouring are all important if the finished product is to be visually balanced. Try to avoid excessively wide boards, which can not only make your cake seem disproportionatly small, but also make piping borders difficult. Boards must at the very least be functional, so make them wide enough, and thick enough, to support and protect your masterpiece.

If you want the cake to be the centre of attraction, keep the board simple, and avoid heavily patterned and multi-coloured coverings, which will draw your eyes towards them, and away from the cake itself.

Having said all that, remember that sometimes you may want to feature a board, in which case, it must be perfectly covered, no matter what medium you select.

Covering with Paper

If you have chosen a paper covering, which is the most common, it must be properly glued on, smooth, and with no tears. Whether you buy or make your own boards, be sure to sand the edges and corners, and you will have far less trouble with tearing. I always round off the sharp corners on square boards (including hexagonal and octagonal), as it makes for a much neater finish. Plastic icing does not lend itself to making sharp corners, so a board with rounded corners will be more in keeping with the whole concept. The simple paper glue which school children use does a good job, provided you don't use so much that it wets the paper and causes it to tear. To smooth the paper on to the top and sides of the board I have pinned a piece of soft cloth over a childs' blackboard eraser. After use, the fabric can be removed, washed of any excess glue and pinned back over the eraser ready for the next time.

Remember when covering petal and heart shaped boards that unless you take precautions, you will have bare board showing on all the inward curves. To remedy this, cover the board with glue, then lay it face down onto the wrong side of the paper. Turn it over and use your eraser to smooth away any bubbles or wrinkles, then lay the board face down again. Cut a small strip of paper for each curve, and glue it to the side and up on to the bottom of the board. Snip the excess paper all round the board, then glue and fold over the two pieces either side of each inserted strip. Finally, glue and fold all the way round, and use the covered eraser to smooth all the edges. On straight sided boards *(square, hexes etc)*, snip round the corners only. Glue and fold them in place first, then fold over and glue the longer side pieces.

Where a wide board covered in paper can make your cake appear to shrink, the same board flooded to match your cake covering will tend to make it seem bigger. This is because there is an unbroken line from cake to board, and nothing to enterrupt your eye as it travels from one to the other.

Board decorations, such as sprays, ornaments, or individual flowers will also be enhanced against a flooded background, and will provide a link to unite the cake and board. You may have noticed that sprays on papered boards often look different to those on the cake — purely because they have different backgrounds. On a flooded board the problem is eliminated.

If you are trying a flooded board for the first time, here are a few hints to help you to avoid the inevitable pitfalls.

Firstly, you must select a board that is thick enough to support the cake without flexing when it is lifted. If it is a tiered board, cover the underside first — either with a self adhesive medium such as Contact, or glue on your choice of paper.

Next cover the board with plastic, such as freezer wrap, remembering to secure it in the centre with a dab of royal icing, and tape it in place on the underside. It is important to use something impervious like plastic, otherwise the board has a tendency to not only transfer smell and taste to the cake, but also suck out and absorb much of the moisture from it. Cover the cake with icing in the usual manner (*don't forget to stick it down with a liberal dab of icing*). Before flooding the board, use a very sharp knife or scalpel to cut away and remove the plastic from around the cake. If you are going to attach ribbon as part of the side decoration, use your dividers to make the line next, and also mark and pipe any embroidery (other than extension and bridgework). Next flood the board, then pipe the base design, be it simple shell border, or intricate bridgework.

For the actual flooding I always make up a special batch of royal icing, adding a few drops of acetic acid, and beating with an electric mixer till it is very stiff. I can't give a reason why, but I have always had more success if I then leave the icing for an hour or two (*longer if you have time*). When you are ready to flood, slowly add water, a little at a time, stirring constantly with a knife, and being careful not to create air bubbles. When the icing will easily sink back to a smooth surface when you stop stirring, it should be ready. Smack the bottom and sides of the bowl to encourage bubbles to surface, and break them with the knife. Place a plastic bag in a cup or tall glass, and fill it with the icing. Tie it off with a knot, or a rubber band. Put the cake on a turntable, snip a small corner out of the plastic bag, and "pipe" the icing on to the board. Start round the base of the cake and continue going round and round as you work your way out to

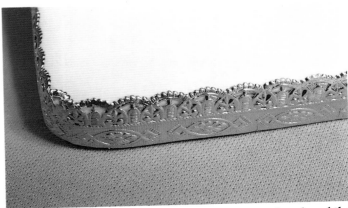

Notice how the gold trimming folds slightly over the edge of the flooded board.

the edges. Unless you have made the icing far to thin, surface tension will stop it from pouring over the sides. Use a clean straight knife to smooth it all over the board. If bubbles appear, dispel them using a chopping action with the knife. Make sure you drag the icing right to the board edge. Tapping the underside will help to level it all out.

If the weather is humid or damp, you can use a hair-dryer to blow the surface dry, but avoid getting the cake hot. the quicker it dries, the shinier the finish will be.

Give the board at least 24 hours to dry, but remember that if it is cold, damp or humid, it may take longer.

When the cake is finished, cut a length of edging - it can be gold or siver trimming, or fancy ribbon - and glue it round the edge with icing. If you choose the paper edging, pre fold the top edge over slightly, before you glue it on and you will have a neater finish.

A large oval and a medium bell both covered in soft cream icing set the mood for this cake. Peach Double Blossom, white Micro Carnations, Eriostemon and soft blue Basic Blossom cascade gently on both cakes. Piped daisies, lace and a simple scalloped border finish it off. See the cover for a different presentation idea.

Inset: Although I have used clear acrylic, chipboard and dowelling (wooden skewers) could also be used to make the support for cakes with central pillars - you just have the extra job of painting them. Push the prepared stand into place, then measure the distance between your cake and the stand and tailor the pillar to fit. Remove the stand, place the pillar on the cake, and replace the stand over it. To ensure stability, the legs of the support stand must go through the cake and rest on the board.

If you were categorising boards, fabric covered ones would be listed between paper covered and flooded ones. As with paper, brightly coloured fabric on wide boards will make your cake seem smaller, whereas fabric that matches the cake covering will tend to make the cake look bigger, as does flooding. Pastel shades are the easiest to work with, and can be relied on to create a soft, romantic look. Fabric covered boards generally exert more visual influence on the total appearance of a cake, so take care in choosing the type and colour. Best results will be achieved if the colour is repeated in the cake decorations, so avoid hues that you know you can't reproduce in icing or ribbons. It is this repetition of colour *(on the board and in sprays or ornaments)*, that has a unifying and harmonising effect on the cake as a whole.

The following hints should help to minimise any mistakes if you are planning to cover boards with fabric.

Firstly, round off all corners on your boards, especially square ones. Heart and petal boards are the most difficult to cover in fabric because of their inward curves, so bear it in mind when you begin planning the cake.

If you aim to use a pale fabric, it may be necessary to paint the board white first, or the colour of the wood will show through, particularly if you use a thin fabric. Of course you can also use painted boards to help with colouring. i.e. Fabric that is brilliant white can be toned down to an icing white if it is glued to a cream board *(and the reverse)*.

Unless you enjoy a challenge, always select a stretch fabric, which can be eased and coaxed around odd shaped boards. Finding the right colour should not be a problem as most fabrics can be easily dyed with a cold water dye, omitting the "setting" instructions as you won't be washing the board. Always thoroughly wash and rinse the fabric first, and read the dying instructions carefully. For a really professional look to your work, dye any ribbons at the same time.

Once the fabric is ready, cut it to size *(approx 7cms or 3ins bigger than the board)*, and lay it face down on a flat surface. Using an aerosol glue, spray the board, then lay it in the centre of the fabric. Lift the board, and smooth the fabric on. Next snip the fabric at approx 2.5cms *(1inch)* intervals all the way round the board. Only cut in about 1cm *(1/2inch)* or so. Hold the board up, and spray the sides of the board, about 3cms *(1-1/4 inch)* on to the base of the board, and on the fabric. Now gently pull and stretch the fabric into place, and press it firmly on to the board. Make sure there are no ugly creases on the sides. The fabric stuck to the base of the board should be smooth for about 1 to 2 cms *(1/2 to 3/4 ins)* before it either has gaps *(where you snipped it in)* or pleats, depending on the stretch and "way" of the fabric, and the board shape.

Cutting away the gathering to leave only that part of the fabric which sticks flat to the board.

Take a very sharp scalpel, and cut away the messy parts, leaving an even, smooth ring of fabric round the board. Make sure you press it down very firmly.

If it is to be a tiered board, then cover the underside as you normally would. One note of warning. Heavy objects left on fabric boards will often leave a faint dent on the fabric, so take care once they are covered.

Wrap the board in a sheet of plastic before sitting the cake on it, remembering to secure it in the centre with a dab of royal icing, and tape it in place underneath. If you fail to do this, there is the possibility that moisture will leach out and discolour the fabric, as well as leaving the cake very dry.

Cover the cake in icing as you normally would, *(don't forget to hold it in place with a dab of icing)*. Do as much of the decorating as you can, before carefully cutting the plastic away from the sides of the cake with a scalpel. This way the fabric stands less chance of being marked in any way.

This cake was designed around one from my previous book. As well as adding an extra tier I used Cooktown Orchids, Violets and Basic Blossom, with fern and lots of pink and white trailing ribbons and loops. The heart theme follows through to the border lace, the outside of which is piped in an 0 tube, and the three leaves in the centre with a 00 tube. A ribbon bow with flooded hearts is the final touch. I used American tins for the cakes as they are generally a prettier shape. They measure 12", 10", 8", and 6", while the box at the top was made off a chocolate mould. The stand heights are 5", 9", 13-1/2", 19" based on the cakes being 2-3/4", 2-1/2", 2-1/4", and 2" high before covering. Allow extra on each tier (cumulative) if your cakes are substantially higher.

Mirror Boards

You may on occasion be asked to decorate a cake on a mirror board. As a rule, the cake is decorated on a conventional board, and then placed on the mirror, so there should be very little difficulty involved. The only point to keep in mind is that mirrors reflect everything, including the underside of cake boards. The most effective way of avoiding an unsightly reflection is to cover underneath any boards that will be directly over the mirror with black paper. (I use Contact). Bring the backing paper as close to the edge of the board as possible, and remember to also use dark cleats. As an alternative to conventional glass mirrors, you may prefer to use acrylic ones. They have the advantage of being much lighter, and a home handyman with a jigsaw can cut it to any shape you desire. Although you should not have to worry about breakage, it does scratch easily, so treat it carefully, and always keep it wrapped when not in use. To avoid scratching the reflective backing stick Contact (or similar) over it. Remove finger marks from the surface by spraying with a silicon polish such as Mr Sheen, and polishing with a soft cloth.

Cleats

Cleats should be both discreet and functional. They are attached to boards to facilitate lifting, and should never be obvious. Avoid covering them with silver paper, which can leave ugly grey marks on treasured table linen. I have found small stick-on rubber door stoppers to be ideal cleats. They are just tall enough, come in white or brown, and have the advantage of being non-slip, which is a boon when delivering cakes.

Pale pink Iceberg rosebuds, Jasmin (with long stamens) and sprays of Basic Blossom and buds combine with pearls and trailing ribbon loops for this different wedding cake. Two white doves hold ribbons leading to two flooded bells, which are the only embroidery on each tier. The cakes are 6" and 10" hexagonal, the pillars 3" high, and the round mirror presentation board is 20" in diameter. See page 44 for how the bells are suspended over the cake.

Allium

These little blossoms from the onion family make really sweet filler flowers. They are naturally white, with a hint of green in the centre, have yellow tipped stamens, and grow in a ball on the end of a fairly thick stem. Of course, you can make them in any colour, and arrange them singly to compliment bigger flowers, or in a bunch as a feature in their own right.

Roll your paste very thin, and cut out the flowers with a hyacinth cutter. finger the edges to smooth them. then lay the flower on your index finger. Use the fluting tool to roll along three alternate petals from the centre out, lengthening as well as thinning them. Lay the fluting tool lengthwise on the remaining three petals, and roll it from side to side, broadening and thinning them. Lay them on soft foam, and use the tip of a very thin fluting tool to drag along the length of the long petals, from the centre out to the tip. Turn them over, and repeat on the side petals. Press a small ball tool on the tips of the wide petals so they curl up slightly. Press in the middle with the ball tool, insert a large stamen in the centre, and stand in florist foam to dry. Be sure to pull the stamen head well down into the icing, or adding the long stamens later will be difficult.

When dry, paint a calyx on the back with thin green royal icing or melted moulding paste.

To finish, chalk a touch of green in the centre, then pipe a dot of royal icing over the centre stamen. With your tweezers, push six very fine tipped stamens under the edges of the royal icing. They should be slightly curved, and level with the centre of each petal, but dont be too fussy. Finally, add a short piece of stamen *(without a tip)* in the centre for the pistil.

Anonymous Flower

Anonymous Flower is a good name for these flowers, because depending on how you colour them, their size, and whether or not they have stamen or pollen centres will decide what bloom they finally represent. They are pictured here in two sizes, with different centre treatments, but the basic construction is the same.

Roll a small amount of moulding paste out until very thin, and cut two pieces the same size for each flower.

Finger the edges of the first set of petals. Lay them on soft foam, and slightly curl the petals, by dragging a ball tool from the tip of each one, in towards the centre. Turn the petals over, and press lightly in the centre with a ball tool.

Finger the second set of petals, and rest them on your index finger. Lay a fine fluting tool lengthwise down the centre of a petal, and roll it from side to side, pressing fairly firmly. Work each petal, then lay them on soft foam, and press in the centre with a ball tool. Paint a small spot of egg white in the middle of the first set of petals, place the second set on top *(alternating them)* and press firmly with the ball tool. Insert a stamen through the centre, and sit in a holed board, or florist foam to dry.

For long stamens: Tape several very fine stamens on to a short length of wire *(28g or 30g)*. Colour thin royal icing to match the flower and paint it on the stem, from just above, to just below the point where the tape meets the stamens. Insert the stem through the centre of the flower, and push it down till only the stamens and no tape shows. Sit in a holed board to dry.

Once dry, paint a small green calyx on the back using either thin royal icing, or if you plan to dip them, melted moulding paste.

Once set, you can add a pollen centre, highlight with chalk, tip the stamens, or dip and steam them, whatever you feel they need to compliment your cake.

Cattleya Orchids, Anonymous Flowers, Eriostemon, and stems of Ivy leaves.

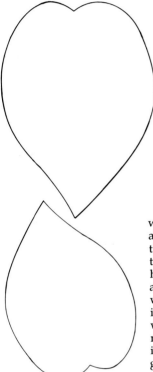

Anthuriums are very easily made flowers, but care and thought are needed when arranging them on a cake. They lend themselves beautifully to clean modern lines, so keep the overall design simple, and avoid a cluttered or tizzy look. The European trend of arranging flowers and foliage in groups and lines, rather than dotting them through an arrangement is ideal for Anthuriums.

Because I make quite a few Anthuriums, I took the time to make moulds on which to dry them. It was simple to roll out and cut craft clay into shape - curling some edges and tips up, others down. I left room to push the wire holding the stamen through, and made them in two sizes. However, if you are not planning to make them frequently, then moulds can be dispensed with, and simply use cotton wool to prop, or rest the sides on.

Cutters are not necessary for Anthuriums, as they are an easy shape to cut out using a scalpel and template. Between five and seven flowers is usually enough for even a large cake spray.

To make the stamens you will need a length of taped wire, and a little piece of fine nylon tulle. Roll a small sausage of moulding paste between your fingers until it is roughly 2.5cm (1inch) long, and about 4mm to 5mm (3/16in) in diameter. Dampen the end of the taped wire with egg white and push it about 1/3 of the way up the length of the paste. Roll the stamen up in the tulle, (it only has to go round once), hold the tulle firmly in each hand, and pull - rather like the way you would pull a toffee paper to unwrap it. When you open up the tulle you will find the stamen is perfectly marked. Trim the base so that where it attaches to the flower it is flat, and give it some character by bending or curling the tip a little, as very few Anthuriums actually have straight stamens. Set aside to dry. The stamens colour up beautifully if you dip them in strong alcohol and food colouring.

Anthuriums are very "plastic" looking, so when the stamens are ready, work a small amount of copha through your paste, and add colouring if desired. Roll the paste out fairly thin, and cut out several shapes. Cover the rest up, and finger the edges of the first one. These templates were cut off miniature Anthuriums, which unlike the large variety, have barely noticable veining. If you have access to a live miniature flower, then you could use it as a veiner, otherwise, fold your flower in half lengthwise, then open it back out to create a centre line. Lay it on soft foam, and run a large ball tool round the edges to curl them up slightly. Melt some of the moulding paste, and paint a tiny amount at the base of the stamen. Insert the wire through the flower about 0.5cm (3/8in) in from the edge and push the stamen into place. Use a clean damp paint brush to blend in the melted paste. Sit the Anthurium in a holed board, and use small pieces of cotton wool to lift the edges, or tuck some underneath to create a curved petal. The stamens should sit at a slightly different angle on each flower, and I also try to curl the sides differently too. Once they are dry, melt some paste and paint a calyx on the back - real Anthuriums don't have them, but they make icing flowers stronger. To avoid the flowers being boring (in a colour sense), I chalk on a touch of colour - a little around the stamen, and just a hint at the tip.

When the flowers are thoroughly dry, steam them lightly to give a waxy plastic look, or you can paint them with egg white if you prefer.

This large oval cake was presented on a round mirror, which reflected the glow from the candles when they were lit. A matching row of silver mirror ribbon added to the ambience. The spray of Anthuriums and small Anonymous Flowers were wired into a European style. The black "gyp" was made by taping together bunches of knobby stamens, and dipping them in colour.

The spray of Anthuriums on this large long octagonal cake was arranged in a true European style. The two-tone leaves are grouped on one side, while the plain leaves add visual weight to one corner. The tiny orchids are grouped in the centre with ribbon loops, and trail up to the top of the spray for continuity. Two rows of ribbon and simple lace over a flooded board give it all an un-cluttered look.

Congratulations
Lisa

Congratulations
Katie

I had always felt that carnations were just too big and heavy for cakes, but with the introduction of the smaller spray and micro hybrids, coupled with better cutters, I feel they are now worthy of inclusion in any cake decorators' repertoire.

As you can see from the outline above, I use the English cutters with individual ready nicked petals. You can also use the cutter for the coriopsis daisy, and nick each petal yourself. As there are fewer petals you may have to add an extra row or two to get the required fullness though.

Start by taping two blank stamens to a stem, then roll out your paste very thinly and cut one set of petals for each flower. These are about the only flowers where I dont finger the edges, as they naturally have a ragged look.

Lay the petals across your index finger, place a fluting tool lengthwise down the first petal, and roll it from side to side, so that the petal is thinned and broadened at the same time as the splits widen. Work all petals, then moisten the centre with egg white and fold them in half. Paint more egg white on the centre, then wrap the petals round the stamens, pressing together at the base. In order that the petals stay tightly around the stamens, hang them upside down in a piece of florist foam which is balanced between two objects.

Once dry, cut another two or three sets for each flower *(it depends how full you want your carnations)*. Work alternate petals as you did for the first set, then turn over and work the remaining ones *(so that some curl up at the sides and some curl down)*. This method gives better separation of the petals and results in a nice fluffy flower.

Lay the the petals on soft foam and press in the centre with a fairly large ball tool. Moisten with egg white and push the wire stem with the first set of petals through the centre and attach the two together. You may have to fold this second set slightly to make them nestle nicely against the first ones, but make sure the two are firmly joined. If your holed board wont keep the petals in place properly, then re-hang them in the foam. Work the third set in the same manner, press in the centre with a ball tool, moisten and add to the back of the others. By the time you add the third set, they will usually sit properly in your holed board to dry. The smaller micro carnations are not as full and fluffy as the sprays, so three sets of petals is normally enough. for larger carnations add a fourth set, worked in the same way, but added when the other petals are dry. Stand them in florists foam, so these last petals flop down a little.

If you are not worried about botanical accuracy, then paint a calyx on the back when they are dry, using either thin green royal icing or melted moulding paste. If the backs are important, paint the calyx carefully, making sure you paint points at the top. Leave to dry, then re-paint, so the calyx is enlarged. Alternately, you can attach a hand moulded calyx.

The horse-shoe which is the main interest on this cake is easily made. Cut out and dry the initial shape, then attach a separately frilled piece around the edge, pressing the join very flat. Mix some thin royal icing and flood the dry part, so the join is covered and it has a "padded" look. Paint the frill with a mix of Silver Snowflake powder and water for a satin effect. The cakes are 6" and 10", and the sprays consist of Micro Carnations, Miniature Cooktown Orchids, Eriostemon and Basic Blossom. Remember to raise the base cake (under the drape) or the folds will hide the side decorations.

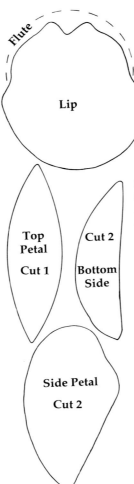

Cattleya are perhaps the most glamorous of the orchids, and always outstanding on decorated cakes. They require few filler flowers around them, so are an economical choice.

The finished flowers can be steamed, so add a little copha or solidified oil to your paste as you work it up.

Firstly form the tongue using moulding paste - the size depends on your cutters, so you may have to experiment first. Roll a small piece of paste between your fingers until it is about 2.5cms *(1")* long, and approximately 3/8 inch in diameter *(or a suitable size for your cutters).* Insert a piece of taped 26g or 28g wire to about half way along it. With the front tip facing you, use the side of your fluting tool to put two dents into it, so it will appear to have three scallops at the tip. Lay it on soft foam, and gently press the end with a ball tool, so that it will curl down slightly. *(see picture for guide to finished look).*

When the tongues are dry enough to handle, colour and roll some paste very thinly, and cut out the lips. Finger all the edges, then generously frill the area at the front, *(where indicated on the diagram).* Paint the

American cake pans were used for these cakes as they generally have a nicer shape. Glamorous white Cattleya Orchids, apricot Anonymous Flowers (with brown tipped stamens) and a few Eriostemon form the sprays, along with pently of ribbon loops. The idea for the unusual butterfly border comes from fellow decorator Rhonda Evans. Pipe the butterfly bodies directly on to the sides of the cake using fairly firm icing, then hold a lace wing in each hand and gently press both into place at once. The cakes measure 10", 8", and 6", and the solid acrylic stands are 21" 14" and 7" (530mm 350mm 170mm). The tiny gold slipper was a keepsake from the Bride's grandmother's wedding cake.

tongue with egg white, and wrap the lip around it. The sides of the lip should meet at the back end, and spread apart at the front, to show off the tongue. If you made the tongue piece too long, or too short, then trim the back now with sharp scissors. Stand in florists foam to dry. You can buy moulds for drying orchid lips, but if you stand them in the foam at a slight angle, they dry perfectly without such aids.

Next cut out the petals, starting with the top one. After cutting it out, finger the edges, then lay it on soft foam. Using a medium ball tool, drag along the length of it, from tip to tip. Sit it in a patty pan tin, or something similar, to dry *(see photo for a guide to drying in shape).*

Now cut and finger the two bottom side petals. Lay them on the soft foam, and using a small ball tool this time, drag it from tip to tip, following the petal's curve. Set in the patty pan tin to dry.

Lastly, cut out, finger, and generously flute the two large side petals. Arrange them in the pans to dry.

When the petals are dry enough to handle, tape some 28g wire very neatly and cut into approx 5cm *(2")* lengths. Melt some moulding paste *(see page 11),* dip about 1cm *(1/2")* of the wire into it, and attach to the backs of all five petals. Depending how you have dried the petals, it may be necessary to shape ➤

some of the wires slightly. Keep a damp brush handy to smooth the melted paste, and avoid big dollops of it. Again, leave to dry.

When the lip is dry, add any chalking or extra colouring required. To get that lovely velvety look, paint the inside lip lightly with water, then dab on scraped chalk with a dry brush -it takes a fair bit of chalk, and a lot of dabbing. Always start with the inside, or palest colour. When you are satisfied, steam the lip to set it. Hold it over the steam in such a way that loose spots of chalk can't intermingle, and keep it well away from the source, or the steam will blow the chalk to where you least want it. Set aside to dry.

To assemble the orchid, start with the top petal. Bend the wire backwards at the very base of the petal, holding firmly so it doesn't break. The secret of not breaking the petals at this point of construction is to use thin wire - too thick wire will result in disaster every time. Next, bend the wires of the two bottom side petals. Hold the three petals into place with the points not quite touching in the centre, and using finger pressure to stick the wires together. If they wont hold together, then a tiny bit of tape round the top near the petals will help. Next add the frilly side petals, followed by the lip. Occasionally, the petals refuse to go together nicely, so try swapping them with others from an orchid you haven't yet assembled, or try adding the lip before the side petals. When you are satisfied, tape all the wires firmly.

To finish, and to stop the petals shifting when you arrange the orchid, melt some moulding paste and paint any exposed wires at the centre of the flower with it. You can also neaten it off by painting green melted paste partway along any of the wire stem which may show in the finished arrangement.

The whole flower can be gently steamed when it is finished, but watch any chalk on the lip isn't blown off and on to the petals.

This method can be used for other orchids, or any flower that requires a "spidery" look to the centre (such as large daisies).

This simple but stunning Christmas cake has been given a floating look with a clever border trick. A row of silver mirror ribbon surrounds the cake base and reflects the board paper. Two rows of lace, (the bottom row flooded) and 2 rows of white ribbon complete the side decorations. The candles and their flames are simply pieces of ribbon glued into place. Holly leaves, berries, 3 Anonymous Flowers, and some silver ribbon loops add Christmas colour to this medium size cake.

Three Christmas Roses, Holly, berries, and ribbon insertion make this 8" round Christmas cake both eyecatching and simple to decorate. A red ribbon bow, with long tails is tucked well down into the arrangement as a finishing touch.

Christmas Rose

I have called this flower Christmas Rose for want of a better name. Made in red and white they are perfect for Christmas cakes, but are just as attractive in other colour combinations

You will need stamens taped on to stems for these flowers, and as they are pure whimsey you can use your own ideas as to what looks best - a few long ones, a bunch of short ones, use a coriopsis daisy centre, corn silk, or as I have done here, sewing cotton. For this method, simply wind the cotton around a finger about 25 times, then slip it off. Bend a piece of wire across the centre, twist tightly, then cut the loops and fluff out the "stamens". Tape the wire, making sure the tape goes up slightly over the cotton to hold it in a nice tight bunch and stops it parting and showing the wire. Dip a brush in food colouring and pass it across the tips, colouring some, but not all the ends. You must remember if you use this method that you wont be able to pull the wire out of the flowers later, so make provisions for it when you design your arrangement.

If you are using an intense colour, such as red, then you will need to steam the finished flowers to get rid of the dusty look, so work in some copha *(solidified oil)*.

Choose your coloured pastes and roll both pieces, keeping the white, or palest colour, slightly thicker. Place one on top of the other and re-roll until it is very thin, and both pieces are well and truly stuck together. Cut out the flowers and finger the edges. To have a pale or white centre with a darker edge, always have the dark colour uppermost as you do this. You will find that the more you work it the more colour is dragged to the edges, and the wider the coloured tips will be. Turn the petals over, and flute all the way round, but don't make it too frilly. Lay them on soft foam and finish shaping the flower by pinching together one or more petals, and pushing the tips or sides of the others over. Make sure that not all the petals are the same, for much of this flower's charm lies in them all being a little different. Press firmly in the centre with a ball tool.

Take the prepared stem and using thin royal icing coloured to match the centre, paint from just above, to just below the top of the tape holding the stamens. Insert in the flower, pulling it well down, so only stamens, and no tape shows. Stand in a holed board to dry

Finish by painting a calyx on the back using thin green royal icing, or melted moulding paste if you plan to steam the backs of the flowers.

Cooktown Orchid

This delightful and easy to make orchid is most commonly known in its deep purple form, however it looks attractive in almost any colour, or combination of colours.

For best results you will need a holed board to dry them on.

Make a tongue for each orchid by rolling a small piece of paste in your hand until it is about 1.5cms (3/4inch) long, and only about 3mm (1/8in) in diameter. Moisten a piece of taped wire and insert it in one end, pushing it about half way along. With your fingers, shape the apposite end, so that looking at it front on, it is roughly triangular, with the tip flattened slightly. Allow to dry thoroughly.

Cut a throat piece for each orchid, and finger the edges to neaten and thin them as much possible. If you wish, use your tweezers to pinch three lines down the centre of the orchid. (Depending on the look I want, I quite often dispense with these). Use your fluting tool, and work around the front lip area. It does not need to be frilled, but worked just enough to make it very thin, and give it movement. Lay it face up on soft foam, and press each side very gently with a ball tool (where indicated on the diagram).

Avoid cupping this area, you only want to give it a slight curl so it will wrap easily round the tongue. Paint the sides of the tongue with egg white and attach the throat. Press the two pieces firmly together at the back end of the tongue, but allow the throat piece to flare away from it at the front. The tongue should appear to be well down into the throat, so if you have made it too long, simply use a pair of sharp scissors to cut the excess away from the wire.

Allow the throats to dry, then for ease of handling, colour them before continuing with the petals.

Once the throats are ready, cut out and finger the petals, and brush on any chalk colour required. Work the three pointed petals first by laying them across your index finger, and rolling the fluting tool firmly across them from side to side. All

Work with Fluting Tool

Press   Press

three petals should be straight with curled up sides. Still using the fluting tool, work around the edges of the remaining round petals, making them as thin as possible, and increasing their size, so that they will overlap the rear petals.

Don't flute them, just give them some lift and movement. Lay the petals on soft foam, and press firmly in the centre with a ball tool. Place the petals on the holed board so that the centre is directly over a hole, then with a ball tool, gently press the middle down into it. (Do this carefully, or the centre will tear). Ease the petals into place - the two front round ones should be over the rear pointed ones. Use small pieces of alfoil or cotton wool to support them if necessary. Paint the back of the throat with thin melted moulding paste, or royal icing, and insert it into the centre of the petals. Dont push too hard or it will tear through. Dampen a fine paint brush with water, and blend the paste (or royal icing) against the petals and throat. Support it with cotton wool if it refuses to stay in place. Once dry, for strength and neatness, paint a calyx on the back using either thin green royal icing or melted moulding paste. (If you have decided to paint your orchids, then it is better to use paste rather than royal icing as it is less affected by the moisture).
If you have used copha in your paste, then finish the orchids by steaming.

Notice how a basically plain cake can be lifted out of the ordinary - in this case by the addition of the long racemes of white Boronia on the top tier. They team beautifully with Cooktown Orchids and Solanum (Eriostemon turned over before pressing in the centre, and with the addition of 4 or 5 stamens taped together and inserted well down into the flower). The round cakes are 11", 8", and 5" and the pillars are 3" clear acrylic.

These cute little orchids are made in exactly the same way as their larger counterparts, with the exception of the tongue, for which I simply use a large stamen. The tiny spots are easy to achieve with the method described below.

If you want the spots only on the orchid lip, then add them before making and joining on the petals.

Work with Fluting Tool

Beryl Gordon helped devise this handy idea for adding spots to flowers.

Because you will need to steam them to set the spots, it will be necessary to use copha or solidified oil in your paste, and in order to avoid burning your fingers, the flowers will need a stem. The rest is easy.

Take a piece of thin paper, and prick a series of small holes in it. Scrape your choice of chalk colour on to the paper. Use a clean brush dipped in water to dampen the area of the flower where you want the spots. Hold the paper over the flower, and shake it gently so the chalk falls through the pinpricks and onto the damp area of the flower. Allow a short time to dry, then steam to set. Small flowers thus spotted can still be dipped for extra colour. Always practice on a spare flower or petal first, and if only one or two petals need spots, then mask those that are to remain clean with a piece of foil or paper to avoid mishaps.

This cake could be called "variations on a theme", as it was designed from a cake in my previous book. This time I used Cooktown Orchids, put stamens in the Eriostemon, made the Basic Blossoms double, and added fern pieces. Using tulle instead of moulded bells kept it looking very light and dainty. The cakes measure 12", 10", 8", and 6". The clear acrylic pillars are all 3" high. See accompanying photo for bell stand.

The bell stand pictured is made from 1/4" clear acrylic tubing, cut to a length of 8" (adjust length if your cake measures more than 2" high before covering). Soften one end over direct heat, and use a skewer or pencil to stretch out the top. Hook the bell wires over it as shown, then fill to overflowing with moulding paste, into which the ribbon and flowers can be inserted. Push the finished stand through the cake to the board beneath.

Mother nature painted this fluffy little daisy in the brightest of yellows, but you will find they look great in any colour. They can be joyful in vibrant colours on a birthday cake, demure in soft pastels atop a wedding cake, or masculine in dark colours for a man's cake. You can have matching or contrasting centres, colour them using chalks, or paint them with food colouring and alcohol. You can also make them with any combination of 1, 2, or 3 rows of petals and stamens, or omit the stamens altogether. However you choose to fashion them, they will enhance your cakes, so let your imagination go, and create your very own "hybrids".

Start with a pea-sized piece of paste, and make the centre by shaping it into a short fat cone. Dip a piece of taped wire in egg white, insert it in the base, then set it aside to dry thoroughly.

If you have decided to add stamens to the centre, roll some paste until very thin, and cut them out next. Use a fluting tool to roll and thin each petal, then with either very sharp scissors, or a scalpel, split each petal at least once, but more if you can manage it. *(The finer they are the better they will look)*. Lay them on soft foam, and with a small ball tool, curl some, but not all, of the stamens slightly. Paint in the middle with egg white, then take the prepared centre piece, push the wire through the middle of the stamens, slide them up and attach them firmly. Arrange the stamens so they ring the centre, but stand a little away from it. Add another one or two rows *(as you prefer)*. Once the stamens have firmed up a little, mix a touch of food colouring with alcohol, and use a fine paint brush to tip each one with colour. If you do this before the stamens are completely dry, the colour is absorbed into the paste, and dries better. Put the centres aside and cut out the petals.

Petals

Cut Here

Stamens and Calyx

These instructions are for three rows of petals, but you can stop at two, or even one row. I generally make the flowers in batches of at least six at a time, which gives the rows of petals a chance to firm between additions.

Roll out some moulding paste until it is fairly thin, cut out the petals, and finger the edges to remove any roughness. Using either sharp scissors, or a scalpel, make two small cuts at the tip of each petal. Lay them across your index finger, and roll the fluting tool firmly across one petal from side to side. With this one action you should broaden the petal, thin it nicely, as well as curl up the side edges. It will also widen the cuts into "V" shapes. Work every second petal *(3)*, then turn over, and work the remainder. You should have three petals convex, and three concave shaped when you have finished. Paint the underside of the centre with egg white, push the wire through the middle of the petals and slide them up and press the two firmly together. In order to have this first row of petals pointing up a little, hang them in oasis foam which is balanced between two objects.

Work the second row in exactly the same way, and attach firmly with egg white, remembering to alternate the petals. This time they should stick out horizontally, so either sit them in a holed board, or stick them into the side of the oasis, and the petals should stay where you arrange them. *(A trick you can use on many other flowers)*.

Work and add the third row in exactly the same way, only stand the flowers upright to dry, so this last row of petals hang down a little. By drying each row at a different angle, you should have good separation between the petals, and a lovely fluffy looking daisy, rather than an unnaturally flat flower. Allow to dry, then colour your flower either with chalks, by ►

A large and medium petal cake, with a central pillar of clear acrylic tube surrounded by filigree, forms the basis of this cake. A ball of tulle, ribbon loops, Coriopsis Daisies, Boronia (with stamens) and Eriostemon (smaller than usual, and with 6 petals) hangs suspended over the cakes (see page 44 for how it is done). The lace and embroidery on the two tiers echo the ball shape, and a single lace butterfly adds interest to the base cake. In this instance the basis of the ball was "dry" or "sec" oasis sprayed white.

dipping or painting with alcohol and food colouring, or by air brush.

If you are aimimg at authenticity (or if the backs will show), then proceed as follows.

Roll a small piece of green paste into a ball, push it up on to the underside of the daisy, and attach with egg white. Roll some more of the green paste out until very thin, and cut three calyx pieces for each flower. Work the first piece either by fingering, or use a fluting tool to make it even finer. Lay it on soft foam, and press in the centre with a ball tool. Paint the ball of paste underneath the flower with egg white, and slide the calyx piece up the wire and press it gently over the ball and on to the back of the daisy. Repeat with the second set of calyx, remembering to alternate them. Thin down the last row, lay it on soft foam, and curl just the very tips with a small ball tool. Slide them up the wire, but leave them sticking out horizontally, with the tips slightly pointing upwards Finally, finish the calyx by painting a small amount of melted paste, or thin royal icing at the base.

If the backs of the flowers are not going to show, then I save time by omitting the above, and painting on a normal calyx.

If you are planning to steam your daisies, do so now, before continuing. For the finishing touch, paint the centre with egg white, spoon on some pollen, then shake off the excess. By leaving this till last, the pollen colour will stay pure, and unaffected by chalks or paint.

Coriopsis Buds

Coriopsis daisy buds are easy to make, and you will see that they are representative of many other kinds of flowers, and therefore will become useful as a basic bud. If made finely enough, and coloured well, they can even be used as a main flower on a small cake. For example, on a christening cake, where they become symbolic of a fresh new life.

Make the bud base by rolling a small pea-sized piece of paste into a ball, and attach to taped wire with egg white. Allow to dry thoroughly.

Roll some moulding paste until fairly thin, and cut out three sets of petals for each bud. Lay the first set over your index finger, and use a fluting tool to roll from side to side on each petal. Paint the bud base completely with egg white, then push the wire stem through the middle of the petals, and slide them up to the underside of the base. Carefully wrap each second petal over the base, so that it is completely covered, then push the remaining four inwards, but leave them standing a little away from the centre. Work the next row of petals, then lay them on soft foam, and press in the centre with a ball tool. Slide them up the wire, and attach with egg white. Repeat for the third set of petals, taking care to alternate them before you press them into place. If you are going to chalk or paint the buds, then allow them to dry, and colour them before adding the calyx.

Buds

When they are ready, roll a small amount of green paste fairly thinly, and cut two rows of petals for each bud. Work them as before, and attach them to the bud, alternating the two rows. Finish with a small painted calyx of thin green royal icing, or some of the green paste melted down.

A large moulded bell hangs suspended above this three tiered round cake. The bell theme is repeated in the 00 embroidery, and the sprays are comprised of Singapore Orchids, Allium, and cream ribbon loops. A light blush of pink on the Allium is picked up in the ribbon around the sides. The cake sizes are 11", 8", and 5", and the clear acrylic pillars are 3" tall. The round mirror base board measures 20" in diameter. See the accompanying small photo for how the bell is hung.

This photo shows how a bell (or ball of flowers) is suspended over a cake. The foot of the stand is grooved and slips over the base board. The side "wings" add stability. It is not possible to give exact measurements, as this will depend on the height and diameter of individual cakes. To put a shine on the cut edges of the clear acrylic rub very hard with a cloth and jewellers rouge (toothpaste is a good substitute). ➤

Everlastings are a very appealing flower, easy to make and suitable for almost any colour and occasion. Many brides will appreciate the symbolism of having Everlastings on their wedding cake.

Roll your moulding paste very thin, and cut two large, and three small sets of petals for each flower. Start with a large set *(cover the rest to avoid drying)*. Place the petals over your index finger, lay a fluting tool along the length of the first petal, and roll it from side to side, pressing fairly hard. Work the other petals in the same manner, so that they are very thin, with the edges curled up. Turn them over, lay them on to soft foam, and use a ball tool to gently press just the tips of each petal. Turn them face up, and paint the centre with a little egg white. Work the second set of large petals in the same way, and lay them over the others, alternating the petals. Using either sharp scissors or a scalpel, split all the petals on the first of the three small sets, *(creating 16 very fine petals)*. Work each half-petal in the same manner as you did the large ones, then with a touch of egg white in between, lay them in place on the main flower. Split the petals of the next set, work them, then lay them face up on soft foam and use a ball tool to slightly cup the tips. Lay them in place on the other petals - not forgetting the egg white. Work the last set in the same way, but curl them a little more. Lay them in place, then with a medium size ball tool, press very firmly in the centre. If your ball tool is too small, all you will do is make a dent in the middle, so it must be big enough to cause the petals to lift up as you press down. Tape a short length of thin wire, bend just the tip at a right angle, and insert it through the centre of the flower. Secure it with a tiny drop of thin royal icing, or melted moulding paste. Set in a holed board to dry. When they are ready, place a tiny drop of thin royal icing in the centre, spoon on some pollen, then shake off the excess.

Finish the Everlasting by painting a calyx on the back with thin green royal icing, or melted moulding paste.

Everlastings are suitable for colouring by dipping in alcohol and food colouring, but if you choose this method, do so before you add the pollen.

* When working the petals, you may find it easier to thin the petals first, before splitting them. They tend to look a little different when finished, but it is better than giving up!

Buds

Double Everlastings and very tiny Double Blossoms decorate this small oval cake (equal to a 6" and 8"). The pillars are 2-1/2" high, and graduated daisy lace makes an appropriate border for the sides.

This medium oval cake relies on its "floating" look, plus two stunning Hibiscus, for impact. A ring of mirror gold ribbon reflects the paper board at the base. (Just a tip - the ribbon has no give, so you will find it easier to keep it laying flat if it is attached with eggwhite when the covering is still soft). Both rows of lace are piped with a 00 tube. Notice that the flooding on the bottom row is not so thick as to hide the veins on the leaves.

Make the bud base by rolling a small pea-sized piece of paste into a ball, and attach to taped wire with egg white. Allow to dry thoroughly.

Roll some moulding paste until fairly thin, and cut out three sets of petals for each bud. Lay the first set over your index finger, and use a fluting tool to roll from side to side on each petal. Paint the bud base completely with egg white, then push the wire stem through the middle of the petals, and slide them up to the underside of the base. Carefully wrap each second petal over the base, so that it is completely covered, then push the remaining four inwards, but leave them standing a little away from the centre. Work the next row of petals, then lay them on soft foam, and press in the centre with a ball tool. Slide them up the wire, and attach with egg white. Repeat for the third set of petals, taking care to alternate them before you press them into place. if you are going to chalk or paint the buds, then allow them to dry, and colour them before adding the calyx.

When they are ready, roll a small amount of green paste fairly thinly, and cut two rows of petals for each bud. Work them as before, and attach them to the bud, alternating the two rows.

Finish with a small painted calyx of thin green royal icing, or some of the green paste melted down.

Buds

The idea for these dainty fern pieces comes from Sue Wells, and I'm sure you will find them as useful as I have. They are ideal for arrangements which need some greenery, but in which leaves just don't look right. (Orchid sprays are a case in point.) The pieces may be as long or short as you need, and either straight or curved. However, if you want curved pieces, it pays to bend the wire stems first.

Use either fine green fabric covered wire, or carefully cover it yourself with florist' tape that has been pulled as thin as possible, so the wire is very smooth (28 gauge is ideal). Cut it into the required lengths, and bend a few pieces for added interest. Take a very tiny piece of green paste, and mould it over the end of the wire to form a small flat leaf. Roll some more paste very very thin, and cut out the fern pieces. Lay one piece on your index finger (cover the rest), and imagining that it is a "Y", place the tip of a fine fluting tool along the length of one of the arms, and roll it from side to side. Work the other arm to match. Paint just the barest amount of water on the leg of the "Y", then lay a prepared wire stem along it, so the arms are just below the leaf. Wrap the leg around the wire, then roll it carefully between your thumb and index finger till the paste forms a thin smooth coat over it. Work it far enough down to cover all the wire up to where the next pair of leaves will be joined on. Continue adding leaves, making sure no bare wire shows between successive pairs. Don't hesitate to pinch off any extra paste, as it is important to keep the stem as fine as possible. For continuity, always lay the wire the same way up as you add each new lot of leaves.

To give the fern stem a natural tapered look have the top leaves laying close to the wire, and gradually fan the rows out till they are at right angles to it.

Once they have dried, the ferns can be dipped in strong alcohol and food colouring to enhance their colour.

In order to give your arrangements a fuller look, try adding a row or two of these leaves to some of your flower stems.

Simplicity is the keynote on this white three tiered round cake. Cream Iceberg Roses and buds are the only flowers. When piping the dropped loops for the border, taper them so that where the bridgework is shorter, the extension becomes narrower, and the angle of the dropped lines stays constant. The cakes are 11", 8" and 5". The twisty acrylic pillars measure 3".

Hibiscus have been made by cake decorators for many years, but traditionally only in fairly vibrant colours, and relegated to feature occasion cakes. The fact that they also come in soft pastel shades, as well as white has largely been ignored. Perhaps after trying your hand at these Hibiscus, you will consider them for a wedding cake.

You will need a mould to form the flower in. The outline is given left and instructions for making moulds are on page 12.

If you have my first book you may already have a Gumpo Azalia mould, which is what I have used.

1st Calyx

2nd Calyx

For the pistil, work your choice of colour into some paste and with your fingers, roll it into a fine stem. Skewer it with a length of thin wire, then re-roll it until it is smooth and even again. The wire should go almost the length of the pistil. With sharp scissors or a scalpel split the tip into four, and slightly spread the pieces. Cut your finest stamens very short, and with tweezers *(and great patience)* insert as many as you can around the the top of the pistil, just below the four splits. You can use plain lengths of stamen, and tip them yourself later if you like. If you have studied fresh Hibiscus, you will notice that the pistils are not always straight, but quite often curved, so keep this in mind *(it also has a softening effect on the look of the flowers)*.

When the pistil has dried, dip the tips of the four split ends in very thin royal icing, then in scraped chalk. Choose a fairly deep colour that will either contrast with, or highlight the rest of the flower. Brush some chalk on the other end of the pistil *(either green, or the colour you have chosen to highlight the veining in)*, and fade it upwards.

Line a prepared mould with alfoil, colour a small amount of paste green, and roll it out fairly thinly. Cut out a calyx, finger the edges, then lay it on soft foam. Use a medium ball tool and press it firmly in the centre. Fit the calyx into the foil lined mould.

Roll your petal paste very thin, and cut out five petals. Cover four to keep them from drying out, and finger the edges of the other one. Hibiscus have very noticeable veins, which you must duplicate to produce a good likeness. Rubber veiners are available, but I prefer to use a fresh flower. Rub a piece of coloured chalk across the veins on the back of a real petal *(the front of a rubber veiner)*, and press it on to the icing to transfer veins and colour at the same time. Dust on any extra colour you require, but be careful not to

spoil the veining. Flute generously round the petal, paint the calyx with egg white, and lay the first petal in place. Work the remaining petals in the same way, placing them in the calyx as you go, and tuck the last one under the first. Make sure all the petals meet in the centre.

Lift the alfoil out of the mould, and sit it on a holed board. Paint a small dot of thin royal icing or melted moulding paste at the base of the pistil, and push it into place. Use small pieces of cottonwool to prop up the corner of each petal so that the finished flower is not too flat. When it is dry, hold it by the wire stem and check that the pistil is firm. If it is not, paint an extra small calyx at the back with thin royal, or better yet melted moulding paste.

If your paste included copha or solidified oil, then steam the flower to set the chalk and give it a natural look. If the back of the flower will show, and you are striving for realism, then there is a second, spiky calyx to add. Roll some green paste very thinly, and cut out a small star shape. Finger and smooth the edges, then push the wire stem through the centre, and slide the calyx up and attach it at the base of the main calyx. This last calyx usually has seven or eight points, but I suggest having however many your most suitable cutter has. They are usually very fine, so you may have to trim them down with sharp scissors.

As the name suggests, Iceberg roses are pure white. The buds have a pale green look, with the tips showing just a hint of pink. Of course, as a cake decorator you can make them any shade you like. Don't be put off by the long instructions, for although they are time consuming to make, one flower is generally enough on a cake.

Firstly, make a centre for each rose by moulding a squat cone shape, and attaching it to a stem of wire or spaghetti. When it has dried, roll out a small amount of yellow paste very thinly, and cut out three daisy shapes for each rose. Thin the petals with a fluting tool, then split each one lengthwise at least once (*twice if possible*). Lay them on soft foam, and slightly cup some, but not all of the petals. Place the three sets of petals one on top of the other, using egg white between, and press lightly in the centre with the ball tool. Paint the base of the cone with egg white, slip the daisy petals up the stem, and press them firmly into place. When they have dried, paint the tips with brown food colouring, and the centre of the cone with egg white. Spoon on some pollen, then shake off the excess.

For ease of handling later, cut out a circle of cardboard, with roughly a 2cm (*3/4in*) diameter hole in the centre. Lay it on soft foam, and build the rose on it.

Cut out a building calyx, finger the edges, and lay it on the cardboard over the hole.

Roll your rose paste very thin, and cut out five of the number 1 size petals. Finger the edges of the first petal, then roll around it with a fluting tool in long sweeps, to give it movement - they should be more twisted than frilly. Work all the petals, paint the calyx with egg white, and arrange them on it, with the points not quite touching in the centre. Tuck a few small pieces of cotton wool under the corners of some petals to give them lift, and avoid a flat concentric look.

Cut out five of the number 2 size petals. Finger and roll the edges, then lay them on soft foam, and press gently in the centre with a ball tool, taking care not to cause the edges to crinkle. Turn them over, and press the very tip of the point with the ball tool. Attach these five petals over the others, using egg white, and alternating them. Again, use cotton wool to lift and hold them till they dry.

Cut out ten of the no 3 size petals. Work the edges as before, then lightly press in the centre with a ball tool. Arrange them in two rows of five, still alternating and propping them up with cotton wool.

Cut out eight of the number 4 petals. Finger and work the edges of five of them as before. Lay them on soft foam, and press just the pointed end firmly with the ball tool. Glue them into the centre of the rose with egg white. They should be standing almost upright, and you may find you need to add or subtract one, in order to fill the centre.

Split each of the remaining three petals in half down the centre, round off the tips with sharp scissors, then finger the edges. Now work the fluting tool very firmly around them, so they twist and curl. These petals then go in the very centre, and you can use all six, or just one or two, as they seem to vary from rose to rose.

1

Cut 5

2

Cut 5

3

Cut 10

4

Cut 8

Paint the middle of the rose with egg white, or a small amount of thin royal icing, and push a centre piece into place. Lift the rose up on the cardboard, and pull the wire stem firmly, so that the centre piece sits snugly among the petals. Place the rose in a holed board to dry.

If the back of the rose will be at all visible in the finished arrangement, then slip a green calyx up the stem, and attach it to the back, followed by a small ball of icing to represent the hip.

Mould a standard bud shape, and skewer it on to a stem. Allow it to dry, then roll out some petal paste and cut out three no 4 petals. Finger and work the edges with the fluting tool. Paint the bud with egg white, then wrap the first petal tightly around it, making sure it goes all the way up the top of the bud. Work another petal, then with egg white as glue, wrap it tightly around the bud, opposite the previous one, making sure that none of the original moulded bud is showing at the top. Any extra icing at the base can be pinched off, and then smoothed over. Work, then wrap the third petal around, but not as tightly. This is the basic bud. You can add one, two or three number 3 petals if you wish, or simply stop at the first two. if you add the number three petals, don't wrap them too tightly. Once you are satisfied, leave them to dry.

When the buds have dried, roll out some green paste, and cut out a calyx for each bud. Finger the edges, lay the calyx on your index finger, and roll the fluting tool from side to side along the length of each point. Lay it on soft foam and press in the middle with a ball tool. Paint the centre with egg white, push the bud stem through it, and slide it up to the base of the bud. Press it into place, allowing some points to hang down, and some to stay attached to the bud. Melt a small amount of the calyx paste (*or use royal icing*) to paint a small hip under the calyx.

Jonquils can be made in really vibrant yellows, or soft creams and peach tonings. Whatever your colour choice, they are easily made and effective flowers for cake decorating. Keep them in mind for Easter cakes.

If you plan to dip the finished flowers to colour them, then remember to work copha or solidified oil into your paste before starting.

For the centre, tape one large rounded stamen, and three of the flat divided ones on to a wire stem. Arrange them so that the round one is in the centre, with the flat ones radiating out from it, and all four close together. Tape them right at the tips, so they will sit low into the Jonquil cup.

Front Petals

Cup

Back Petals

Colour the paste for the cup, roll it out thinly, and cut out two or three cups. Finger the edges, then flute round them, so they are very thin. Lay on soft foam, and cup them by rolling a ball tool round and round, starting on the outside, and working in towards the middle. Set aside, then colour and roll out the petal paste. Cut one set of both petals for each flower. Finger the edges of the wide set, lay them over your index finger, place the fluting tool lengthwise down the centre of a petal, and roll it firmly from side to side. Work the other two petals, so that all three are thin, with the edges curled up. Place them face down on soft foam, and with the tip of the fluting tool, drag down the centre of each petal. Turn them over, and gently pinch together just the very tip of each petal. Work the narrow set of petals in the same way. Moisten the centre of the wide petals with egg white, place the narrow ones on top, alternating them, then press lightly with a ball tool. Paint egg white in the centre, position the cup, and press it in place with the ball tool. Paint a tiny amount of thin royal icing, or melted moulding paste, at the back of the prepared stamens, and insert the wire stem through the centre of the flower. Push the stamens down till they are flat against the cup. In order to have the flowers dry with the petals flared slightly backwards, I place them in egg cartons *(as below)*, but remember to dry some with the petals forward to add interest to the finished arrangement. It is also wise to lay some down to dry, so they will lie more naturally later.

Unlike daffodils, which are flat at the back, Jonquils have a fairly long tubular extension which you can add next, or ignore if the backs of the flowers won't be showing If you dont want a realistic look, when the flowers are dry, paint a calyx on the back with thin green royal icing or melted moulding paste. If you are aiming for realism, melt some of the moulding paste, and paint the extension on the back of the flower. Use a barely wet brush to smooth over where it joins the petals, then leave to dry. Finish by painting on a tiny green calyx of melted moulding paste or thin royal icing.

When they are thoroughly dry, dip them for really vibrant yellows, and steam them to add a natural look.

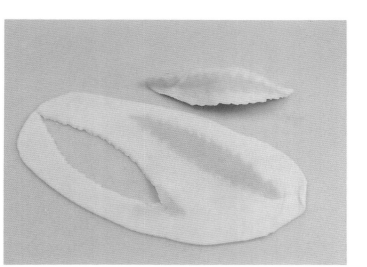

Although you will occasionally make an arrangement that looks good without leaves, most are enhanced by their addition. They do not have to botanically match your flowers to look correct, rather you should rely on a leaf that either compliments or contrasts with the shapes in your arrangement. The latest floral trend is to use two or more different shaped and coloured leaves at a time.

To make leaves you will need cutters, plus either a plastic leaf, a rubber mould or a fresh leaf from the garden to use as a veiner. Roll your paste thinly, and cut out the leaf shape. Lay it on the mould you have chosen, and press firmly to transfer the pattern of the veins to the paste. Press very firmly round the edges in order to make them as fine as possible. Twist or curl some leaves, then leave them to dry.

You will find it very convenient to make a lot of leaves of several different types at one time. Make them all a soft green, as they can then be tinted to suit your arrangements later. To colour them you can use chalks, an airbrush, or dip them. If you decide to dip them they will need stems. Small leaves requiring only short stems can have stamens attached. For heavier leaves, or longer stems you will need fine taped wire. To attach the stems, first melt some matching coloured moulding paste *(see page 11).* Dip the tip of the wire or stamen in the melted paste, and lay it along the centre back of the leaf. If the backs of the leaves will not be visible in your finished arrangement, then they can be left as is. If they will show, then use a slightly damp brush to smooth over the paste, so that it blends into the leaf, and looks like a large vein once it has dried.

A simple spray of pale Jonquil, buds, ribbon loops and dark green leaves adorn this cake for "Nanna". A bright border of matching Jonquil lace surrounds it, and the gold of the board is picked up in the piped wording.

Two Tone Leaves

Two tone leaves can be used to great effect in highlighting the flower colours in a bouquet. Ready made leaves can have chalk brushed on the tips, or can be painted. To do so, use your dipping solution, and paint the end of the leaf nearest the stem in one colour, then dip the tip in another. As you spin off the excess liquid, the two colours should blend. If you are not satisfied with the result, then use a brush to merge the colours together before you twirl them.

Bi-colour leaves can also be made by using two different cutters, or by a little hand moulding. Colour up two lots of paste, and roll out the paler, or central colour. Cut out some odd shapes using either a special cutter, or part of another irregular shaped one. Roll out the darker, or main colour, and with a little egg white, stick the paler pieces on it. Roll the paste again, so that it is all prefectly flat, and the second colour pieces have blended in. Now cut out your leaves. The paste that is left over can be tinted back up to the darker colour and re-used. If you don't have a cutter suitable for the pale pieces, roll small balls of paste in your fingers, and pull them into odd shapes by hand.

Most leaves look better for being steamed *(page 14)*, or painted with an edible shine, as they will then add another texture to your arrangement.

Miniature Daffodils

These cute little "daffies" can be used as filler flowers, or as feature flowers in their own right. You will find they look their best if the trumpet is a deeper or different colour to the petals. You can tint them by dipping *(see page 15)*, but remember it will add extra colour to the trumpet as well as the petals, so bear it in mind when colouring the paste.

Colour the paste for the trumpets, roll it until it is fairly thin, and cut out several pieces. Use a fine fluting tool to work round the edges, so they are extra thin. Lay on soft foam, and cup the trumpet with a small ball tool, by running it around in a circular motion, starting at the outside edge and working in towards the centre. A final firm press in the middle should produce the desired effect. Make all the trumpets, then colour the petal paste, roll it out very thin, and cut a set of petals for each one. Lay the petals over your index finger, and roll the fluting tool along three alternate petals, working from the centre out. This will make them extra fine as well as a little longer. Next lay the fluting tool lengthwise down the middle of each of the untouched petals, and roll it from side to side, so they curl up a little on the edges. Finish these petals by pinching just the very tips together.

Paint a small spot of egg white in the centre of the petals, and put the trumpet in place. Lay on soft foam, and press gently in the centre with a ball tool, so that it attaches properly, and makes the petals move a little *(your daffies will be very boring if they all have flat and even petals)*. Insert a stamen through the centre, and set in florist' foam to dry.

Once they have set, paint a small green calyx on the back using either thin royal icing or melted moulding paste.

When they have completely dried, you can dip them if you wish.

Apricot Nerines, Anonymous Flowers, Eriostemon, stems of Ivy leaves and wide ribbon loops accompany the Tulle Church on this hexagonal cake. The very simple border is designed to take nothing away from the top decorations. The cakes are 10" and 6". The stand holding the top tier measures 14" high.

erines can look quite spectacular on a cake, and as they are fairly easy to make, are worthy of consideration by cake decorators. Although they are clumped together in nature, I find that they have far more impact when allowed plenty of space in an arrangement.

The most common colour is a rich deep coral tone with brown tipped stamens, but like most other flowers, they have been hybridized and now come in plenty of other colours. You will need a mould to make it in *(see page 12)*, and the shape is indicated at left

Tape eight or nine fine stamens on to a stem first. The stamens with coloured stems are best, and you can always colour the tips to suit the flowers yourself. Use the full length of the stamens, and once they are taped, slightly dampen them to about half way up from the bottom, and roll them between your fingers so they stick together. Leave them to dry, then gently fan the tips out slightly.

Line a prepared mould with alfoil, and cut out a calyx from the same colour paste as the flower. Work the edge of the calyx with a fluting tool to make it as fine as possible, lay it on soft foam, and press in the centre with a ball tool. Fit the calyx into the lined mould.

Roll some more paste until it is nice and thin, and cut out six petals for each flower. Cover up five of them, and finger then flute the edges of the first one. Lay it on soft foam and drag the tip of your fluting tool down the centre of the petal, from tip to tip. Moisten the inside of the calyx with egg white, and put the first petal in place. Make sure it is firmly stuck to the calyx, and curve the petal over the edge of the mould gracefully.

Work the remaining petals in the same way, placing three in the calyx first, then the next three over and between the first ones. Again, make sure that they are all attached properly.

Melt a little of the paste *(or colour some thin royal icing to match)* and paint a small amount round the tape holding the stamens to the stem. Push the stem through the centre of the flower, and pull it down till just the stamens show, and none of the wire or tape. If your mould doesn't have a hole in the base you will have to lift the alfoil and flower out to do this. Sit aside in a holed board to dry.

When the petals are thoroughly dry, carefully dust a darker shade of chalk colouring along the centre of each petal. It is best to do this while the flower is still in its foil cup, as the petals will be supported and less inclined to break.

To finish the Nerine, remove it from the alfoil carefully, and paint a small amount of melted moulding paste *(or thin royal icing)* over where the calyx and petals meet. blend it carefully with a slightly moistened brush, so that once dry, it will not be obvious that there is a calyx at all. With some melted green paste, or thin royal icing, paint a little hip at the base of the flower. Once thoroughly dry, you can brush on some of the darker chalk colour, fading it off as it goes up the back of the petals. Handle the finished flowers with great care, as their shape makes them susceptable to breaking.

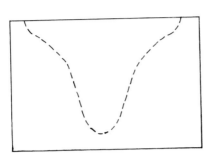

I used Nerines, Heath, Ivy stems and Eriostemon for the spray on this large oval cake. The slightly different look of the Eriostemon is achieved by turning them over before pressing the centre. Lots of cream ribbon loops, plus slim candles finished the top, and simple lace and embroidery adorn the sides.

If you become bored with making Everlastings, turn them into Paris Daisies. They should naturally be yellow, but as a cake decorator, you are in charge of colouring, and you can make them as you please.

Roll our your moulding paste very thin and cut two sets of petals and three circles for each flower. Start with a large set *(cover the rest to avoid drying)*. Place the petals over your index finger, lay a fluting tool along the length of the first petal, and roll it from side to side, pressing fairly hard. Work the other petals in the same manner, so that they ae very thin, with the edges curled up. Turn them over on to soft foam, and use a ball tool to gently press just the tips of each petal. turn them face up and paint the centre with a little egg white. Work the second set in the same way, and lay them over the others alternating the petals.

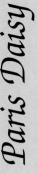

Take the first of the circles and using sharp scissors or a scalpel, cut small nicks all the way round it. Flute the circle carefully, so that it will have a ruffled look, but with individual petals obvious. Paint the centre of the large petals with egg white, and add this first circle. Work the remaining two in the same way, and glue them in place with egg white. Press firmly in the centre with a medium ball tool - it must be big enough to cause the petals to lift up as you press. Bend just the tip of a taped wire at a right angle, and insert it through the flower. Secure it in place with a tiny drop of thin royal icing, or melted moulding paste. When they are ready, paint a small calyx on the back with thin green royal icing, or melted moulding paste. Once set, put a drop of thin royal icing in the centre, spoon on some pollen, and shake off the excess.

These daisies look great if you make the fluffy centres a slightly darker shade than the outer petals.

Make any buds required in the same manner as described for Coriopsis Daisies.

A butterfly theme runs through this cake - from the flooded one at the top (perched invisibly on a piece of nylon fishing line), in the 00 piped embroidery, and finally around the base as lace. Singapore orchids, plus Eriostemon with a touch of pink make up the sprays. The gold of the 2 wedding rings is repeated on the boards, and through the gauze ribbon among the flowers. The cakes are 10" and 6", and the clear acrylic pillars 2-1/2" high.

Singapore Orchids have become one of the most popular flowers used in bridal bouquets, and justifiably so. Although creamy white is the colour most often used, they come in many variations, some bright and beautifully spotted, others more subtle. With the trend towards co-ordinating all aspects of a wedding, there comes the need for cake cake decorators to be able to reproduce these delightfully exotic flowers.

Singapore orchids are cream, with green touches, rather than white, so colour your paste cream first. The green touches can be chalked on last. If you plan to paint the colour on last using food colour and alcohol, then you should start with white. For the best results see your local florist for a fresh orchid. You will find it easier to shape and colour your own orchids if you have a real life one to copy from.

To make the tongue, mould a small piece of paste into a tiny carrot shape, approximately 2cms (3/4 inch) long. Bend the to end over at right angles, and finger it so that looking at it front on, it is roughly triangular shaped, with the front slightly flattened. Pinch the two bottom corners and pull them down slightly. Tape a short length of wire, and bend the tip back on itself *(for better grip)*, dip in egg white and insert into the back of the tongue *(see photo)*. Allow to dry thoroughly.

Once the tongue is dry, cut out a lip, finger the edges, and very lightly flute where indicated on the diagram. Don't frill it, but rather just add a little "movement". Take your tweezers, and pinch three lines down the centre of the lip *(as indicated on the diagram)*. A real orchid has five lines, but you may find it hard to do, and the finished look doesn't warrant the extra difficulty. Lay the lip face up on soft foam and press the two sides with a ball tool *(where shown on the diagram)*. Paint the pointed end of the tongue *(which is called the sac)* with egg white, then wrap the lip round it, matching the point of the lip with the tip of the sac. The sides of the lip should stand away from the tongue at the top, but be pressed smoothly on to the sac. Pinch off any excess paste, or stretch it down to fit if necessary. The front of the lip should stick straight out, or at the most, only slightly curved down. If you have studied a fresh orchid, it will be easy to achieve a natural look for this part. Stand the finished lip in oasis foam to dry - if you stand it just right it will dry at the correct angle.

You have just made the hard part - the rest is easy!

While the lip is drying, make a square of alfoil approximately 7cms (3ins) square to support each orchid as it dries.

with Fluting

Work **Tool**

Press Press

Lip Cut 1

Cut 2

When the lip is completely dry, cut one set of back petals, and two front side petals for each orchid. Finger the edges of the back petals, making them as fine as possible. If you wish to have a veined look, then press a piece of dried corn husk on to each petal at this stage. Lay the petals face up on soft foam. and drag a ball tool from the centre, up to the tip of the top petal. Do the same with the two rear side petals, but follow their natural curve. Lay the petals on the piece of alfoil. Finger the front side petals, vein them if you wish, then work lightly round the edges with your fluting tool to give them movement. Lay them in place over the back petals with egg white between to stick them firmly. Take the dried tongue and lip and paint the sac with egg white. Push the wire through the centre of the petals and alfoil, and bring them up so you can wrap the pointed end round the sac. Use the foil to support the petals while working this part, and pinch off any excess. The two sides should meet at the tip of the sac, and gradually spread as they go up towards the lip. Fold the foil round the sac when you are satisfied with it, and use it to support the two bottom petals. They should follow the line of the lip, with the tips curved slightly downwards. By cutting or bending the supporting foil you can have the remaining petals sit in whatever position you wish. Try to make each one a little different - half buds are made by lifting all the petals forward. Stand the orchids in oasis foam or a holed board to dry. ➤

The geometric shape of this three tiered hexagonal cake is emphasised by the angled lines of lace on the sides. The look is softened by sprays of mauve Singapore Orchids, Eriostemon, and Basic Blossom. A few pearls and a Tulle Bell complete the picture. The cakes are 10" 8" and 6" and the clear acrylic pillars are 3" high.

To finish the orchid I paint a calyx at the back using matching coloured royal icing *(or melted moulding paste)*, which adds strength. If you are chalking your flower, then lightly dust the throat, sac, and inside of the petals with soft green. New, freshly opened orchids are quite green, fading to white, then cream as they age, so vary the colours of your orchids as well as the sizes. A touch of pale honey brown on the tip of the tongue adds a realistic touch to flowers which are meant to be older.

If you are painting your flowers, then mix a hint of pale green food colouring with strong alcohol, and paint it on the throat, inside petals, and sac. Make a pale cream mix using yellow, caramel brown, and alcohol, and wash it liberally all over the orchid, including the parts already painted green. If it appears blotchy, spin the orchid by the wire stem to flick off any excess. Once dry, the orchid can be lightly steamed to give it a natural waxy look *(provided you have used copha in your moulding paste)*. Steaming also helps to set the colour on chalked flowers.

Violets

Violets come in several different forms, and though they all have four pointed and one round petal, the way they each curl and twist does vary. These violets are meant to be representative of several different species, rather than a precise botanical copy of one. Remember when making violets, that as well as the best known purple ones, they also come in pale mauve, pink, and white.

If your paste recipe does not include Copha *(solidified oil)*, then add a small amount as you work up your paste. Roll it out until it is very thin, and cut out the violets. Finger the edges, then lightly flute the round petal - it's not meeting to be frilly, just give it a little movement. Next, shape the pointed petals by laying the flower on your index finger, and roll the fluting tool from side to side along the length of each one. Turn the violet over on soft foam and press the round petal gently with the ball tool. Curl the top two pointed petals by stroking the ball tool from the tip, in towards the centre. *(You can vary the violets by pressing the side petals with the ball tool instead of the two top ones).* Turn it over, and press in the middle. Insert a flat yellow stamen in the centre, and arrange the petals by lifting the round one forward, and pushing the top two backwards *(or however you feel they should lay).* Sit in a holed board or florist foam to dry. If the stamen won't sit flat against the lip of the violet, push the stem into the side of the florists foam with the flower facing down.

Once dry, paint a small green calyx on the back with either thin green royal icing, or for preference, melted moulding paste.

When the calyx has dried, paint three fine lines in the centre in a deep colour. *(These are optional.)* Next, melt a small amount of Copha *(solidified oil),* and paint the stamen and the very centre of the flower. Once the Copha has re-set, dip the violet to colour it. The stamen will be unaffected by the colour, and the centre will stay white.

Leaf

Leaf

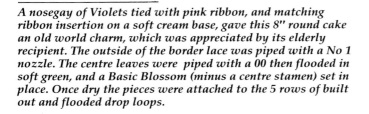

A fluffy cream Iceberg Rose, three buds, and a flooded butterfly are the simple adornments that make this white oval cake suitable for any occasion. The cream ribbon insertion takes your eyes through the spray, and on to the butterfly. When piping the dropped loops for the extension, taper them, so that as the bridgework gets shorter, the extension becomes narrower and the dropped lines all remain at the same angle.

A nosegay of Violets tied with pink ribbon, and matching ribbon insertion on a soft cream base, gave this 8" round cake an old world charm, which was appreciated by its elderly recipient. The outside of the border lace was piped with a No 1 nozzle. The centre leaves were piped with a 00 then flooded in soft green, and a Basic Blossom (minus a centre stamen) set in place. Once dry the pieces were attached to the 5 rows of built out and flooded drop loops.

Notice that even though the leaves and small flowers are either grouped or in lines, rather than spotted through it, the whole arrangement is still in harmony.

Having perfected icing flowers, the next hurdle is arranging them to their best advantage on a cake. Any flower will be easier to arrange if it has a stem, but not everyone wants to push wire stems into a cake, and neither are all cake decorators capable of wiring together a spray.

One of the easiest solutions is to use spaghetti as stems. If you can't get the green variety, it is easily painted with food colouring. The only drawback to spaghetti is that it can't be bent, so sprays sometimes appear rather stilted.

Another remedy is to cut out a small circle or oval of plastic from an ice cream or margarine container. Cover it with a small mound of icing, and arrange the flowers over it. When finished it can be lightly attached to the cake with royal icing, but easily removed when the cake is cut. If you require a cascade effect, then you will need to have a few flowers on the cake which are not connected to the basic spray. Provided the stem wires are straight, and were not bent at right angles during the making of these flowers, then they can be removed. Hold the flower by the calyx, grip the stem with a pair of pliers, and using steady pressure, pull out the wire. These flowers are then safe to put directly on the cake. Remember, never cut off a piece of wire stem right at the base of a flower. Wire should always be very obvious, to avoid the possibility of it being accidentally swallowed.

For those who have the floristry knowledge and skills, then a wired spray which rests on the cake is the answer. If you are not expert in the field of wired sprays, then perhaps a few brief pointers will help to improve your technique as described below.

Always start with the leaves. Form them into the basic shape that the arrangement is to take, then lay them on the cake, to check that the shape and size is correct. All the leaf wires should be held together in one place, usually referred to in floristry as the "holding point". Everything you now add to the arrangement - be it flowers, ribbon, pearl stems or whatever must be attached at the holding point.

After the leaves, add a few ribbon loops, as these will hide much of the mechanics of the spray. Next add the main flowers. Don't push them down too far into the spray, or they will lose their prominence when the filler flowers are added.

Study the spray before adding the smaller flowers, so that they can be put in place without a lot of shifting around. As a general rule, you will find it best to wire the smaller blooms into little sprays before adding them.

Never twist wires as you make the spray, or it will be nearly impossible to pull out a flower you wish to shift. The taped wires should hold together with finger pressure, but it is acceptable to use tape to keep the stems together at the holding point.

Once you have some confidence in your floristry ability, try a European arrangement. Instead of having a spray with mixed flowers dotted through it, add them in groups, or lines of colour and form. Even the leaves are used in groups of different shapes and colours. (*A typical European arrangement has a selection of long, oval, and heart shaped leaves*). This style of floristry is very modern, and also very economical in its use of flowers, relying mostly on form and colour for impact, rather than numbers of flowers,

Whether you choose a traditional or European style arrangement, always remember that the spaces you create in and around it are just as important as the arrangement itself.

A large oval and a medium bell both covered in soft cream icing set the mood for this cake. Peach Double Blossom, white Micro Carnations, Eriostemon and soft blue Basic Blossom cascade gently on both cakes. Piped daisies, lace and a simple scalloped border finish it off.

These marzipan cuties are a great hit at Christmas time, as well as being fun to make. With just a little imagination, they can be made to suit many other occasions. Try adding a bib and/or bonnet for christenings, or a wild party hat for new year and birthday celebrations. Lady mice can be indicated by simply adding a large bow between the ears, and gentleman have a bow tie or mous(e)tache of course. For a comical look an extra long tie trailing in front is tops. For wedding mice, she has a little tulle veil, and a posy of flowers in front, he has top hat and tie. As well as on a cake, they can be used as place markers, by sitting them on small gum paste plaques. My Christmas mice all have licorice allsorts wrapped as parcels beside them, but holly would be just as effective.

You can use plastic icing or moulding paste for these mice, but the best results will come from using good quality marzipan which has been well worked.

Backward as it sounds, I make the ears and tails first. The tails are obvious - just a thin tapered piece of paste, curled so it will sit beside or in front of the mouse. The ears are made by rolling paste into a small ball, laying it on soft foam, and cupping with a ball tool. Pinch together two sides, and leave them to dry. Take a piece of marzipan, work it up well and roll it into a ping pong size ball for the body. Lay it on a board, and roll it with the edge of your palm until it resembles a fat carrot. Next use a ball (or anger) tool to push in the eye sockets. Remember, much character shines through the eyes, so angle the sockets to suit the look you want.

As you push in the sockets, so the nose will tend to tilt up. Use a small knife to press a line from the nose tip down to where the teeth will be. Sit the mouse on his prepared tail to dry.

At this stage I have added whiskers made from the hairs of a cheap brush which was cleaned with boiling water, but black stamens serve as well. If the mice are for children, it is best not to use either, but paint them on later. If you are airbrushing for extra colour it can be done now, or wait until it is dry enough to handle, and chalk on highlights.

Attach a tiny oblong of white paste for teeth, press it flat with your finger, then cut down the centre with a scalpel to form two teeth.

Add the whites of the eyes either by piping them in royal icing, or using little balls of white plastic icing. Colour some plastic icing red, and form it into a peaked dunces cap. Sit the cap in place and fold it over at a jaunty angle. Pipe white "fur" round the cap base, and push the ears into place. Pipe a fluffy ball on the tip of the cap, and add a black nose, and pupils to the eyes. Your christmas mice are ready, but be warned, all who see them will be captivated, so be prepared to make plenty! Merry Christmouse.

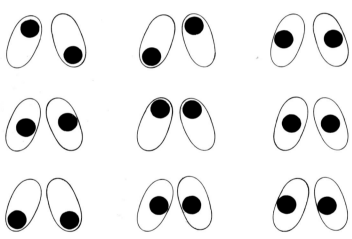

A Christmas Mouse surrounded by a holly wreath forms the centrepiece of this 7" round cake. The base border was built out with 4 rows of dropped loops which were brush flooded, then topped with a further row of red piping. Two rows of red ribbon enclosed by red piped embroidery finish the sides. I made a mouse plaque for each guest at the table where this cake took pride of place.

On this cake Silver Snowflake powder chalk was mixed with a little water and painted on the half bells to give them a pearly finish. Anonymous Flowers, two-tone Holly leaves, berries and a few silver ribbon loops added to the Christmas feeling. The border design was created with drop loops. Working from left to right, pipe four rows, each one a little longer than the last. Brush flood them, and once dry, overpipe with green. Add the holly and berries last.

The moulded bells pictured on pages 27 and 45 are both made using the same technique, as would be much smaller bells.

First obtain a mould - mine are all off Christmas decorations, but you can usually find a selection of shapes and sizes at cake decorating outlets. As it is the inside of the bell that is used, any brands stamped on the plastic, or rough parts must be smoothed away. A sharp knife, followed by sandpaper is pretty effective. In order for the bell to balance upside down I also cut away the hanging loop at the top. Wash and dry the bell thoroughly, then using a spare piece of paste, rub all over the inside as hard as possible. Check the paste to see if it has been discoloured at all, and if not, your bell is ready for use. If the paste is discoloured, rub the inside as hard as possible with a soft cloth, then check again with the paste.

Coat the inside of the mould with a fine film of copha *(or solidified oil)*, followed by a generous dusting of cornflour. Take a good handful of paste, and work in some copha *(or solidified oil)*. You will find it far easier to make these bells if your paste is fairly soft, so use either very new paste which hasn't had time to firm up, or work a little water into older paste. Once it is thoroughly worked up, form it into a ball, cup it in one hand, and push the thumb of the other hand into the centre of it. With your thumb still in the middle, use your fingers to gently pull at the paste as you turn it round. Try and keep the outside as smooth as possible. When it is about half the size of your bell mould, dust the outside generously with cornflour, then drop it into the bell. Take a spare piece of paste, place it in the corner of a small freezer bag, or wrap a little plastic over it, and use this as a tool to rub the inside of the bell. Keep moving your wad of paste round and round, always forcing the bell paste towards the lip of the bell. Cut away the excess paste as it forms over the edge, and continue pressing and smoothing until you are satisfied that it is thin enough. Check to see that the paste is not sticking to the bell, and cut off any that remains hanging over the lip. It really doesn't matter how thick the main body of the bell is, as long as the bottom edge is nice and fine, so run your plastic covered wad of paste round and round the edge until you have it as smooth and fine as possible.

If you have decided on a scalloped edge, then make yourself a cutter out of a wine bottle lid *(as I do)*, and press out the scallops. Use your wad of paste to smooth them off once they have been cut. Sieve some cornflour or icing sugar, and pack inside the bell with it, pressing it down firmly as you go. Level it off at the top, then lay a small board or piece of heavy cardboard across it, and turn it over. Gently remove the outer mould, and check to see that the bell you have made is smooth and flawless. If it is flawed, replace the mould, empty out the packing, and press and work it until you feel you have rectified the problem. This way, your mould is ready for immediate re-use, and you don't have to wait two days for a bell to dry, only to find it is un-usable. *(Be warned however, if you use lumpy icing to pack your bell, you will end up with a dented one)*.

When it is partly dry, use a pin or piece of wire to make a hanging hole at the top. If you are planning to decorate the bell with flowers, you can also make holes in the sides in which to insert the stems, which is neater than attaching them with dots of icing.

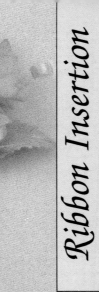

R ibbon insertion is an easy way to add colour to the top or sides of a cake. On the top of a cake, it can visually stretch a small arrangement, and so becomes useful for "rush jobs". Where the sides of a cake are not perpendicular, or are not smooth, and a ribbon would not sit flat, then insertion is the answer *(Bell cakes are a case in point)*. With the right tools and knowledge, it becomes very quick and easy. All you need is an arrowheaded ceramic tool, tweezers, and dividers. Plus your ribbon of course. I have found the results are best if the cake has been iced for two or three days, so it has had time to set properly.

For the top of a cake, make a paper template, lay it in place, and work around the edge of it. For a side decoration, cut a strip of paper which you can wrap round the cake to indicate the height at which you require the loops.

Decide what size loops you want, then double the measurement, and set your dividers *(eg for 1/4in loops set the dividers at 1/2in)*. Making only tiny pinpricks, step off the dividers round the template. Next, reset them to half the size, and go round again, putting one point in an existing mark, and making a new one with the other. In this manner you will always have an even number of holes, and evenly set loops, with no gaps when you reach the end.

Next, take the arrowhead tool, and holding it perpendicular to the cake, make a slit on each pin-prick. For a neat finish, make each slit just long enough to accommodate the width of your ribbon.

Cut your ribbon into lengths the same size as the first set of marks *(that is, twice the length of the required loops)*. Use your tweezers to sit a piece of ribbon in every second slit, then still with the tweezers, go round again and push the other end into place. Use your finger to gently rub each loop flat as you go along.

Just a small tip - when purchasing an arrow-head tool, look for one with a curved blade on the reverse end. They are invaluable for scraping royal icing mistakes off the sides of cakes, or tucking in behind curtain borders to remove dropped strands. To keep my arrowhead sharp, I rub the blade between a fine piece of folded sandpaper before and after each use.

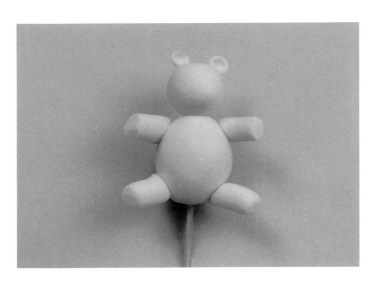

The Teddy Bear pictured on page *71* is very simply made -all you need is a small length of taped wire, moulding paste, thin royal icing, and some very fine coconut *(pollen)*.

It is best to start with the Teddy's body as this will determine his finished size, so first mould a piece of paste into a rotund oval. Take another piece of paste, roll it into a ball, then pinch out a short snout, and slightly flatten the area above it where the eyes go. Roll two tiny pieces of paste into balls, lay them on soft foam, and press with a small ball tool to form the ears. Attach them with egg white, and use the ball tool to press them firmly into place. Join the head and body with egg white, then push a length of taped wire, *(spaghetti or a toothpick will also work)*, up through the body and into the head. Make sure the wire is long enough to leave a decent hand hold at the bottom.

The Teddy's arms and legs are just rolled lengths of paste, with one end cut straight across, and the other end cut at an angle. Join the angled ends to the Teddy with egg white. Keep the arms and legs fairly short, but don't worry too much about smoothing over the joins, as they will be hidden by the "fur" later. Allow to dry.

Colour some very fine coconut by mixing it with scraped chalk. For pastel shades, first mix the chalk with either cornflour or potato flour.

Hold the Teddy by the wire and paint him entirely with very thin royal icing, then roll him in the coconut. To create a nice dense coat of "fur" you need to really press the coconut on, so I found the best way was to lay plastic wrap over my soft foam, and spread the coconut on that. It enabled me to press fairly firmly without the fear of breakage.

If you want your Teddy two-tone, then paint and coat the parts that are to have the darkest colour first, allow it to set, then paint and coat the paler portions.

Colour a tiny amount of thin royal icing black, and paint little dots for eyes and ears. If you have some poppyseeds, then they can be used to good effect. All you need to finish off is a jaunty bow, and a cake to sit him on!.

If you tire of Teddys, then make a rabbit. The only difference is the head, which apart from the long ears is more egg shaped, with the pointed end forming the nose. However, you must be careful when coating rabbits as the ears are easily broken off.

What could be cuter for a christening cake than these fluffy teddies. Anonymous flowers, Violets and very tiny Double Blossom, with a few pieces of fern, accompany them.

This Dolly Varden basket holds a grouped arrangement of tiny Rosebuds, Anonymous Flowers, Double Eriostemon, and a line of small Double Blossom at the back, plus some fern and a fluffy teddy. The border design around the medium oval cake was achieved by masking out the rest of the cake with strips of paper, and air brushing just the exposed area. Once the paper was removed 00 embroidery in a matching colour was piped on.

Welcome
Nathan and
Ashley

Welcome
Peter David

O ver the years it has become possible to purchase plastic ornaments to suit almost any cake theme. However, a great number of cake decorators live in country areas away from specialist shops, and it is not always practical to send off for special items. Others, like myself, simply enjoy the challenge of creating their own ornaments. Over the next pages you will find instructions and ideas to help you be creative too.

These ornaments are all made with *"tulle"*. Perhaps here I should make a small correction. What is used is not strictly tulle, but *COTTON MOSQUITO NETTING*. The reason it is referred to as tulle is simple - how many brides would accept an idea for a cake if you said you were making the the top ornament out of mosquito net? Tulle simply sounds nicer, and the title has stuck. All the ornaments described are made to the same principle - that of stiffening the tulle, drying and shaping it, then covering it with finely piped cornelli work.

Unfortunately I can't give precise measurements for all the ornaments, as not everyone will have the same shapes and moulds that I have used. I do, however, recommend making a paper pattern for each item first, to avoid wasting the tulle and as a time saver for later repeats.

This cake was designed for a 21st celebration with a beach party theme. The shell lace border, and the tulle shell echoed the pattern on the invitations. Double Blossom and Eriostemon kept it suitably feminine.

Tiny peach rosebuds and small mauve Anonymous Flowers fill a tulle Dolly Varden basket on this medium hexagonal cake. The flowers are arranged so they appear to be laying along the basket as if just picked, and the stems which overhang are made and put in place separately. Ribbon loops hide the point where stems and flowers meet.

T ulle ornaments are remarkably easy to make, providing you follow a few simple rules, the most essential of which you will find here.

When greasing moulds, always use white shortening, such as copha or lard - never butter, which will stain the tulle. Only a light coat is required, then place the the prepared mould in the refrigerator till ready for use.

When stiffening the tulle always use *HOT* solution - reheat any mixture that has cooled down.

Always pat off any excess mixture with a towel, kitchen paper, or a barely damp sponge, to avoid sugary build-up on the dried ornament. However, if you find your dried tulle has clogged with sugar, simply use a pin to break the pieces out. It is tedious and time consuming, but better than wasting an ornament.

A damp sponge is best for patting the tulle into place on a mould.

Once dry, the warmth of your hand is normally enough to release an ornament from its' mould, but should this fail, a pin slipped under the tulle here and there will usually shift a stubborn one.

The ornaments which are cut out of flat tulle are easier to manage if you tie pieces together at the corners. It is a simple matter to thread a length of white cotton through matching holes on either piece, tie with a double knot, then cut off the loose ends as short as possible. This way, joins once cornellied will be invisible and your ornaments will not only be stronger, but will appear to have been made in one piece. Take care not to pull the knots so tight that the pieces overlap, they should always just meet.

Stiffening tulle is an incredibly sticky business, so I usually gather up all my moulds and make as many shapes as possible at the one time. The tulle shapes will last indefinitely if stored in a dry place, and you will find them very handy for the *"cake that should have been ready yesterday"* for if you have an ornament your cake is half done!

I could fill a book with instructions for various tulle ornaments, but because tastes are so different many would never be used. Instead, I suggest you invent your own. Any filigree patterns you may have *(such as a horse and coach or bassinet)* can be adapted by just following the methods on the following ideas.

Finally, a word to the wise. Always try to work or pipe tulle against a dark background, otherwise you will find yourself, quite literally, going crosseyed!

T he recipe for stiffening "tulle" is simple, provided you remember that it is not nylon tulle that you work with but COTTON NET.

Mix three parts of ordinary white sugar *(the kind you stir into your tea)*, with one part of water. Heat the mix - either in a microwave or on the stove - until it comes to the boil. Remove from the heat and stir until the liquid becomes perfectly clear. Use while still very hot, and reheat if it cools.

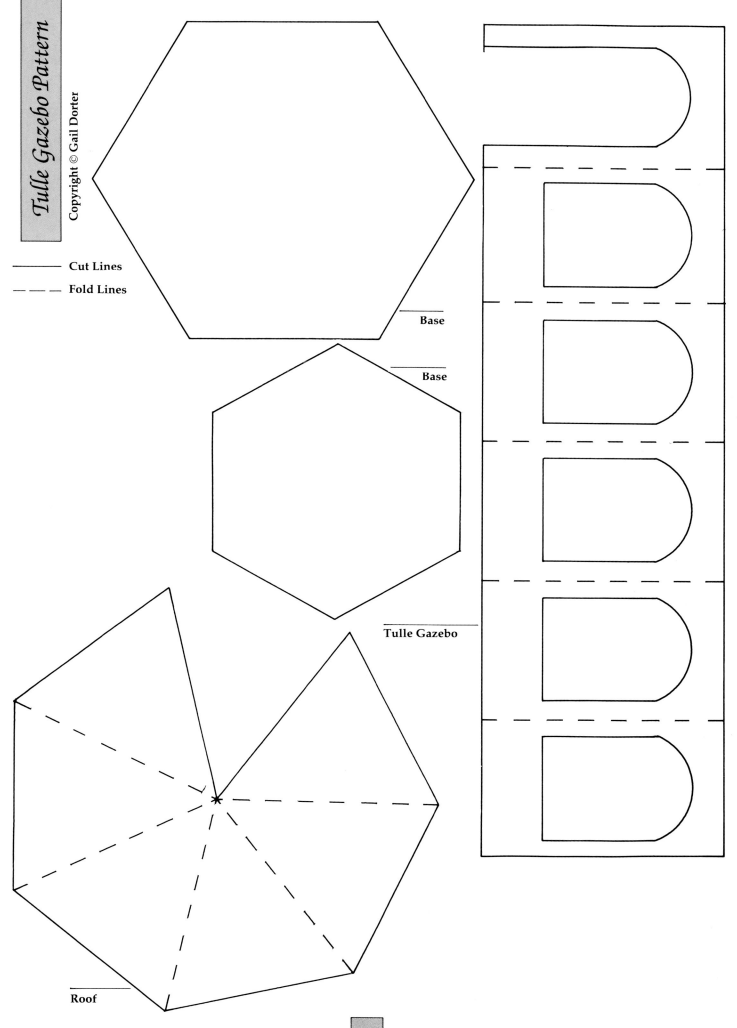

Tulle Gazebo Pattern

Copyright © Gail Dorter

——— **Cut Lines**
– – – **Fold Lines**

Base

Base

Tulle Gazebo

Roof

77

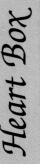

My heart box is made over a small china ornament, but there is no reason why a larger plastic box couldn't be used - the instructions would be just the same.

To make a pattern for the base of the box, measure *AROUND* the sides first, then measure from the top, *DOWN* the sides, and underneath to what would be the centre of the underside. Allow enough to overlap at the centre back, plus a little extra for shrinkage. For the lid, make a pattern to the same shape, with enough left to fold over the sides and under a little way, plus shrinkage.

Lightly grease the mould and place in refrigerator for a few minutes. Cut out the tulle using your prepared pattern, and place in the stiffening mix. Once it has had time to thoroughly soak, start by removing the bottom piece with tweezers, and blot off any excess mixture. Wrap the tulle round the mould, starting at the back, and allowing it to protrude a little above the top edge, and overlap at the join. Once you have it around the mould, use sharp scissors to make upward cuts in the tulle which is hanging down from the sides *(see pictures page 81)*. Turn the mould over, and one by one, fold in these pieces to form the base of the box. Press it all firmly on to the mould with a barely damp sponge, then leave to dry.

Next remove the top piece of tulle from the stiffening, pat off any excess mix, and lay it over the lid. Turn it over, and pull the side pieces in, towards the centre. If the lid is curved, you will have to pull and stretch the tulle to avoid creases. Fold the tulle into the middle, and weight it down - I use small coins, which are removed half way through drying.

Once dried, trim off the excess from round the top of the base and the edges of the lid before releasing them from the moulds.

Finish the ornament with a fine cover of piped cornelli, and add centre decorations before securing the lid in a half open position. Use the smallest possible amount of paste to hold your centre decorations in place, or the box will look heavy, instead of light and delicate. For a quick strong result, use melted moulding paste to hold the lid in place.

Everlastings grace this simple but elegant 2 tier cake. The heart shapes of the 10" and 6" cakes are repeated in the border lace and tulle jewel box. The open lid exposes a single gold wedding ring among ribbon loops and small flowers. Very tiny Basic Blossom and Forget-me-nots finish the sprays. The stand holding the top tier fits snugly into the curve at the back of the base board, and measures 8" high.

I have used an ordinary Vegemite jar for this pretty ornament, but any jar that suits the size of the cake you will be sitting it on can be used, the instructions would be the same. In this case, the same jar makes both the top and botton pieces, so it is convenient to have two jars ready.

To cut a pattern, measure **AROUND** the jar first, allowing for overlap at the join. Then measure from the centre of the bottom, across, and about half way up the side. For the lid, cut a circle that will go across the bottom, and about 2.5cms *(1inch)* up the sides.

Lightly grease the jar(s) and place in refrigerator. Cut out the tulle using the paper patterns, drop it into hot stiffening mix, and allow time for it to be properly absorbed before removing the piece for the base.

Blot off any excess stiffening, then wrap the tulle round the jar, pulling it so it is a tight fit, and overlapping it at the join. Use a pair of sharp scissors to make upward cuts in the excess tulle hanging from the bottom of the jar *(see pictures opposite)*. It should take about 8 cuts. Turn the jar over and fold these pieces in, one on top of the other, to form the base. Pat it all firmly with a barely damp sponge, then set it aside to dry.

Remove the lid piece from the stiffening, and blot off any excess mixture. Turn the jar base up, and lay the tulle over it. Stretch a strong elastic band around the jar and over the tulle, then gently pull the ends of the tulle till the part above the band is wrinkle free.

When both pieces are dry, use the warmth of your hand to remove them from the moulds, and trim to the height you require. Bear in mind the size of any ornaments you may be putting inside the box before you cut it down to size.

Finish with cornelli piped with a 00 tube, and lay the lid of the box against it in a casual manner. You can fill the box with any of the things that you would find in an ordinary jewel box - engagement ring, eternity ring, wedding rings, string of beads, rosary, gold cross, or even a cameo brooch or pendant. You can mould your own out of paste, or purchase real jewellery, but whichever you choose, take care to see that it is secured in the box with the minimum amount of icing possible.

Coriopsis Daisies (with 2 rows of petals and stamens), small Anonymous Flowers, and Heather (forget-me-nots glued on to stamens with melted moulding paste) surround this round Tulle Jewel Box. The lid leans casually to one side, exposing an eternity ring nestled among ribbon loops and small flowers. Coloured embroidery and a matching board spray complete this medium oval cake.

Keeping the tulle for the lid wrinkle free and in place with an elastic band.

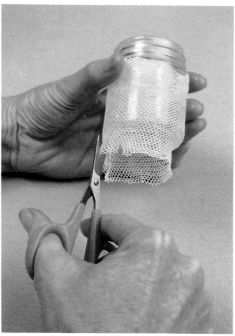

Making upward cuts in the excess tulle hanging from the bottom of the jar.

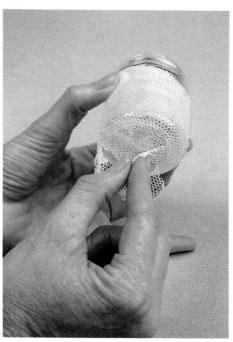

Folding the cut pieces in on top of each other.

Tulle Church

Many times I have considered using a church ornament as the centre piece on a special wedding cake. Invariably the idea was discarded when I found I hadn't the time *(and patience)* for a filigree church, and paste churches always look too heavy, with sides that never seem to fit. This tulle church really is the answer. It is incredibly easy to make, and although it looks delicate, it is surprisingly sturdy. It is quick to make, with the added bonus that you will need fewer other decorations to accompany it. It can be used on the top tier *(this pattern will fit on a six inch cake)*, on a large single wedding cake, or as a presentation board ornament.

Firstly cut out all the pattern pieces, and use them to establish how big a piece of tulle you will need. *(You can join the two side pieces together and cut them out as one, but must take extra care when folding, or it wont sit square when finished).* Try to be as economical as possible, but remember that there will be some shrinkage. The tulle needs to be stiffened and dried first, so you will need a flat surface that can be greased on which to dry it. I use a piece of acrylic board, but just as easy is a kitchen bench top. Do it last thing at night, and it will be dry by morning, with minimal inconvenience to yourself and family.

While the tulle is soaking in stiffening mix, lightly grease the flat surface you have chosen to use. Remove the tulle once it is thoroughly saturated, and blot off any excess with a towel or damp sponge. Lay the tulle out flat, pulling evenly at the edges till you see that all the little holes are the same shape - you don't want some pieces to have oval holes while other parts have round ones. Once it looks fairly even, take a piece of freezer paper or waxed lunchwrap, lay it on top of the tulle, and proceed to flatten it all nicely. Check again to see that it is all even, with the edges as smooth as possible *(some bunching and puckering is inevitable)*, then carefully remove the top paper and allow the tulle to dry thoroughly.

Once it is dry, carefully pin the pattern pieces firmly against it and cut them out as accurately as possible. ➤

A Tulle Church is the centre of attention on this 10" cream hexagonal cake. Cymbidium Orchids, Anonymous Flowers, and Heath, all in soft pinks and mauves, plus a few fern pieces and cream ribbon loops set it off to perfection. Taper the dropped loop base for the border so that it becomes narrower as the down pieces become shorter, then the angle at which they fall will remain constant.

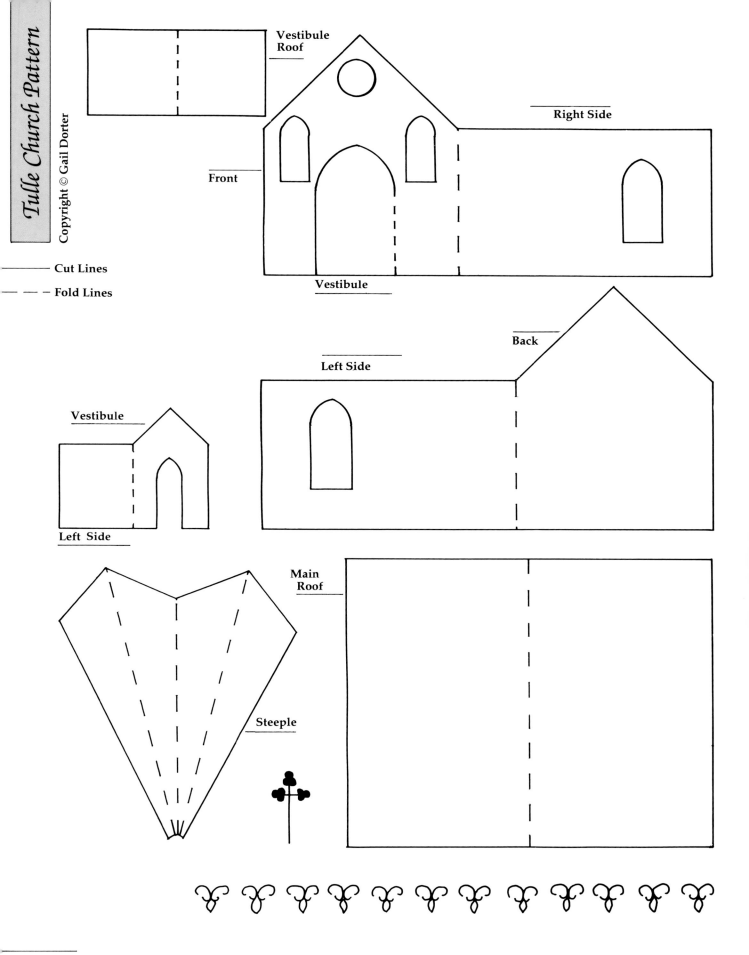

Tulle Church Pattern

——— Cut Lines

— — — Fold Lines

Vestibule
Roof

Right Side

Front

Vestibule

Back

Left Side

Vestibule

Left Side

Main
Roof

Steeple

Tulle Church

The Vestibule can be transferred to a 'Long Side if preferred.
The left and right sides can be joined and cut out in once piece.

Commence building with the piece marked **BACK**. Keep the tulle and the pattern together, and lay them both down on your work area, with the tulle uppermost, and the fold lines on the pattern clearly visible. Lay a ruler where indicated by the dotted line, and fold the tulle upwards, to form the left hand side of the church. Take the piece marked **FRONT**, and using the same method, fold forward the side of the vestibule, then fold the main side piece back. These two pieces should now form the basic church, with one side of the vestibule. If you find you have folded a piece the wrong way - forward instead of back or vice versa - just refold it, taking care to keep it a nice sharp fold.

Next take the vestibule piece, and fold along the dotted line, so it will form the front and left side of the entry.

Using white cotton thread, tie these three pieces together at the corners. You may find it helpful to use a needle, and only tie the knots tight enough to bring the edges together, don't cause them to overlap. One double knot on each corner is usually enough to hold it all in place. Cut off the loose ends as short as possible.

Fit a piping bag with a 00 tube, fill with royal icing, and cornelli over the church, leaving bare a small area above where the roof of the vestibule will meet the church front. When you come to corners, make a point of going back and forth from one side to the other. This will not only add strength, but give your corners a nice neat finish.

While the piping on the main church is drying, fold the roof piece for the vestibule, and attach it. Cornelli the roof and across to the area of the church front which was left bare. As before, this will help strengthen and hold the roof on.

Next fold the main roof piece, and attach it with a few well placed dots of icing along the top edge of the side pieces. Now fold the steeple. You must be very careful to fold it precisely where marked, and try to leave a tiny hole at the top where the cross will later be inserted. *(if it doesn't work out, you can always cut one)*. Tie the steeple edges together with a double knot at the base, cut off the loose ends, and sit the steeple on the roof, towards the front of the church. If you have cut and folded it correctly it will sit perfectly, if not you may have to cut and adjust it. Take the time to see that it is straight from both the front and side views, as a crooked steeple will spoil all your previous good work. Start to cornelli from the tip of the spire downwards. Carefully work back and forth across the join at the back, as well as from the steeple to the roof to avoid a *"tacked on"* look. Continue over the whole roof.

Once dry, you can add lace pieces to the eaves if you so desire. Finally, crown the steeple with a piped cross by insterting the end of it down the hole you should have left at the tip. The two little dots on the leg of the cross will stop it from going too far down into the steeple. Secure it with a dot of royal icing. I usually add these finishing touches after the church is on the cake and any other decorations are in place, as they are easily dislodged.

You can site the church directly on the cake, or make a stepped pedestal for it to stand on. Simply roll some fondant, and cut out two or three pieces, each a little bigger than the last. Smooth off the edges, and allow to dry on a flat surface. Once dry, stick them together, one on top of the other, to form stairs up to the church. Before making them however, look at both the church, and your cake, and decide on whether your pedestal should be the same shape as the church, or whether perhaps it should reflect or compliment the shape of the cake. Once finished the pedestal should be attached only lightly to the cake, so that it can be easily removed and retained as a keepsake, or perhaps as the top decoration on a future anniversary cake.

Depending on the shape of your cake, you may prefer to have the vestry on either the long or short side of the church. Either way it is easy enough to superimpose the pattern on a different side, and cut it out accordingly.

[I]f you have some tulle ready stiffened, then you can easily make this sleigh. With a few holly leaves, and the minimum of flowers, you will very soon have a completed Christmas cake.

Stiffen some tulle using the method described for either the church or gazebo *(see pages 76 or 82/84)*. While it is drying, flood the runners, and put them aside to dry also.

Roughly cut out the side pattern, and two pieces of flat, stiff tulle. For accurate reproduction, pin all three together and cut along the lines. Cut out the base piece. Note that it is longer than necessary. This is because it can be frustrating trying to get the corners all meeting exactly, so I have made provision for the base to protrude up beyond the sides. It can be trimmed off after you have knotted the two sides and base together in six or seven places. Use a threaded needle and cotton to tie the knots, and make sure you go through a complete circle of tulle on each side, so the cotton wont pull through as you tie the knots. Be careful not to make them too tight or the seligh will twist out of shape.

Cornelli the sleigh with a 00 tube and royal icing, taking care to pipe back and forth across the joins in a random fashion, so they will be invisible once finished.

If the runners are dry they can be attached now. Rest the sleigh on something which is 13mm *(1/2in)* high and stick the runners in place so that they will just touch the ground, and are both level. I find melted moulding paste is ideal for this.

When the runners are firmly in place, rest the sleigh on something taller, so that there will be no stress on them as you decorate it.

Fill the sleigh with ribbons and flowers, or holly leaves and berries. Perhaps you would prefer little squares of foam wrapped as parcels, but whatever you choose, keep them lightweight.

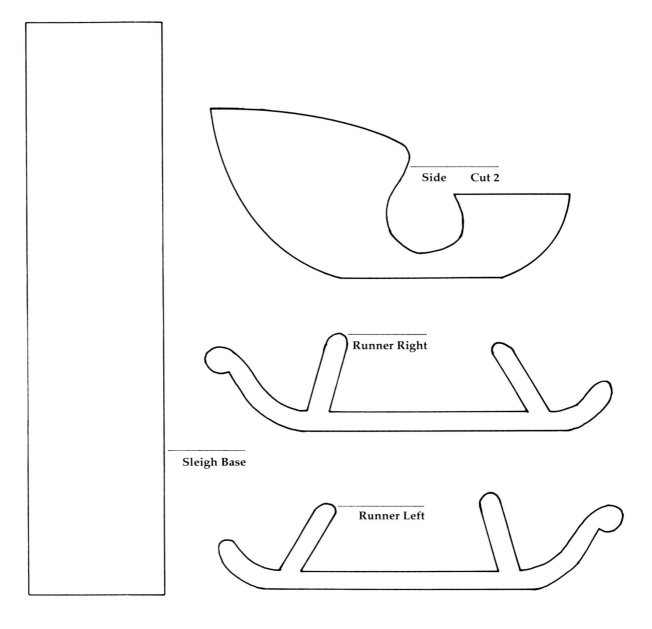

Side   Cut 2

Runner Right

Sleigh Base

Runner Left

Tulle Sleigh

Tulle Pram

The pram makes a delightful ornament for a christening or first birthday. You can also delete the wheels and handle, add two carry handles on the sides and it becomes a carry basket.

As you can see it is made out of a single piece of stiff flat tulle. *(Follow the instructions for stiffening given under either the church or gazebo).*

Cut out a paper pattern of the pram but dont go right to the edges. Pin the tulle over the pattern so you can see the fold lines through it. Cut both pattern and tulle out together for a perfectly accurate shape.

Leave a pin in the centre of the pram. Where you see marked "front fold", lay a ruler or similar on the dotted line, and fold the tulle upwards against the ruler. Repeat on all the dotted fold lies, always folding upwards.

Tie all the sides together with a double knot. Make sure you go through holes that match up on opposite pieces, and dont pull the knots so hard that it causes the sides to overlap, or the pram will be misshapen. Tie each fold of the hood to the side of the pram separately.

Once you have cut away all the loose ends from the knots you should have a complete carry basket, with neat invisible joins, and ready to cornelli with a 00 tube and royal icing.

When piping the cornelli, remember to go back and forth randomly across both sides of each join for a neat and strong finish.

If you wish to make a pram. before piping the cornelli, you should fit the handle. I have used 26g wire neatly covered with florist tape. The wire fits down the front corners of the pram and folds back over the top If you measure it carefully you will find it sits in place without needing any icing to hold it. However, as you cornelli over the pram you can lightly touch from the pram to the handle if you wish to be doubly sure of its staying put.

Pipe the wheels as you would for lace, and once dry, remove and attach them carefully. Arrange any flowers on the cake first, and place the pram last of all, as the wheels are very delicate.

* If you dont like the appearance of the wire, it can be camouflaged by diluting royal icing with water till it is thin enough to paint on the handle without dropping off it. You can also use the wire as a pattern and mould a handle out of paste.

Tulle Slipper

The slipper has been a symbol on wedding cakes for generations, but made in tulle it is daintier and undated.

Provided you have a mould *(either use a chocolate mould or separate both sides of a full plastic slipper)* it is easy enough to make.

Whether you make the slipper in one to two pieces depends on the actual shape of the mould you are using. I was able to coax mine out of one piece, but if you have difficulty, simply make the bulk of the shoe in one piece, and the heel in another. Overlap any joins carefully, and once piped with cornelli they will become invisible

Grease the mould, then cut out a rough pattern in tulle. Soak it thoroughly in hot stiffening, then remove with tweezers. Blot off any excess mixture, and stretch it over the outside of slipper. Tuck the spare tulle over and into the inside, weighing it down to keep it in place *(I use small coins for this).*

Repeat for the other side and allow to dry. When ready, cut off all the excess tulle exactly on the edges of the mould before using the warmth of your hand to release them. Tie the two pieces carefully together with double knots of white cotton. Take care to have the two sides just meeting and not overlapping.

Finish with fine cornelli piped with a 00 tube and royal icing. As you pipe, make sure you go back and forth across the joins in a random fashion to strengthen and hide them.

Cut Lines

Fold Lines

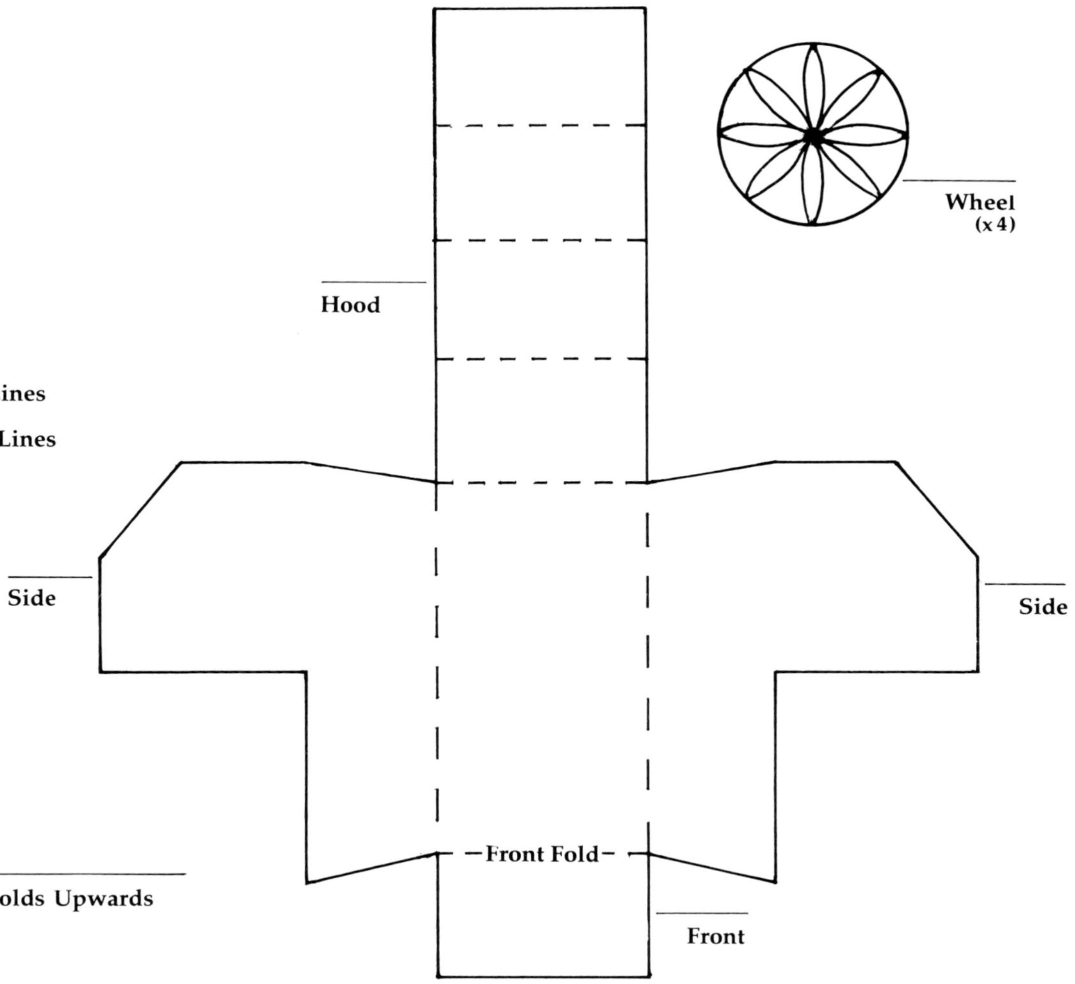

Wheel
(x 4)

Hood

Side

Side

All Folds Upwards

—Front Fold—

Front

Tulle Pram

P lastic swan moulds are available from cake decorating shops, and I have used one of these to make my swan. While it is not impossible to use the plastic swan intact, it is far easier if you first break it in half, along the join. To this end, when buying your swan, look for one that has been poorly glued, and separating the two pieces will be easier.

With a lot of patience you can make the swan in two pieces, but it is far simpler to make it in four, even though it takes a little extra time.

Make a rough pattern for the main body, and another for the neck and head. In both cases, allow for shrinkage, and for the tulle to go over the body and tuck down inside the swan.

Grease the swan pieces, and place in the refrigerator while you cut out the tulle from the pattern. Place just the body pieces in hot stiffening mix, and after they have absorbed enough solution, remove the first one with tweezers, and blot off any excess moisture. Wrap the tulle round the mould, easing it just a little way up the neck. Turn the swan over, and fold the tulle down into the mould. Use a few coins or similar to fill the swan and keep the tulle in place. The weights are necessary, as you will have to pull the tulle fairly tight to encourage it to follow the contours of the swan. When the outside of the body is dry, remove the coins to allow the inside to dry. Repeat for the other side.

When these pieces are completely dry, add the neck and head pieces, overlapping at the join. This part is not easy, but remember that it is also not impossible, and just keep easing and folding till it is right. I don't bother with the beak, as it is easier to pipe or mould one and add it on later.

Once the neck pieces have dried in place, trim round the edges of both pieces, and gently remove them from the moulds. Tie the two sides together at four or five strategic places, using white cotton and a simple double knot. Don't pull so tight that the pieces overlap - for a perfect invisible join the two sides should just meet. You may find it easier to use a needle when doing this part.

Use a 00 tube to pipe cornelli all over the swan, and finally add either a piped or moulded beak, and a cere *(the coloured flesh immediately above the beak)*. Fill the swan with a few very fine ribbon loops and tiny flowers, or maybe even a ring. Whatever you use, attach it with only the smallest amount of icing possible, or it will show through, and the swan will look chunky, instead of light and elegant.

Purple Coriopsis Daisies with 3 rows of petals and 2 rows of stamens.

Pink Coriopsis Daisies with 3 rows of petals and 1 row of stamens.

Yellow Coriopsis Daisies with 4 rows of petals and no stamens.

Umbrella

Perhaps the easiest ornament of all to make. I was fortunate enought to find a plastic umbrella to use as a mould, but you can also use a toy ball to achieve the same result.

If you are using a ball as a mould, grease about half the ball, and put it in the refrigerator to set. Cut a circle of tulle, and immerse it in hot stiffening solution. Allow it time to asborb the mix, then remove with tweezers, and blot off any excess. Stretch the tulle over that part of the ball which has been greased. Pull it well down past the line of the umbrella shape, so that any creasing or puckering can be cut off later. Stand the ball in a container to stop it rolling while the tulle dries. Once it has dried, ease the tulle off the ball, and cut it to shape. You should use a pattern for this, choosing either scalloped, straight, or a convex edge.

If you have an umbrella shaped mould it is just as easy. Cut a pattern to fit across the umbrella and tuck underneath, with allowance for shrinkage. Grease the mould, and store in the refrigerator while cutting out and soaking the tulle in hot stiffening. Remove the tulle from the mix and blot off any excess. Stretch the tulle over the umbrella, and fold it underneath. Turn the umbrella over and fill the upturned shape with coins or something similar, to keep the tulle tight. Once the outside has dried, remove the weights to allow the inside to also dry.

When the whole thing is completely dry, cut it neatly round the edge, and use the warmth of your hand to release the finished shape from the mould. Insert a handle, either moulded out of paste, or made by taping a piece of 20g wire first with florist tape, then ribbon. Secure each end of the ribbon with a tiny spot of glue, and when it is set, bend one end round a pencil to form the handle.

If you want ribs on your umbrella, pipe them in place first, then finish with fine cornelli between them.

Moulding Paste

25og icing sugar (8 ozs)
30ml water (1 oz)
2 scant teaspoons gelatine
1 rounded teaspoon liquid glucose

Sift icing sugar into a bowl. Measure water into a small bowl or cup and sprinkle with the gelatine. When it has been absorbed stand in a saucepan of hot water and dissolve gently. Once it has completely dissolved add the glucose. When the liquid is clear and free of any lumps add it to the icing sugar, stirring with a knife. Store the mixture in a plastic bag and seal in an airtight container. The mix needs to stand for about eight hours before use.

Stiffening

3 parts sugar
1 part water

Stir over heat until mix boils. Remove from heat immediately and continue stirring till all sugar grains have dissolved. Use while hot. Store in sealed container in refrigerator. Reheat before next use.

If you have a microwave, then you can make very small amounts and use it fresh each time (1 tsp of water to 3 tsp of sugar).

Edible Shine for Leaves

A   *1 part Gum Arabic (Acacia Gum)*
      3 parts water

Put water in a small bowl or cup and sprinkle with the Gum Arabic. Stand in a pot of water and boil until the gum has dissolved. To use, keep on a gentle boil, and take the leaves to the stove. The mix dries very quickly, so you must work deftly and fairly fast. Use a brush wide enough to cover the leaves so they are done in one stroke. If you want to chalk leaves first, it must be done when the modelling paste is soft, and rubbed well in, otherwise when you paint on the gum you will wipe off the chalk at the same time. Store in an airtight container in the refrigerator and re-boil it when next required. It is advisable to make only a small amount at a time.

B   *1 tsp gelatine*
      1 tsp liquid glucose
      2 desertspoons water

Put the water in a cup or small container and sprinkle over the gelatine. When absorbed, stand in a pot of water and heat until dissolved. Add the liquid glucose, and stir well. Keep the mix warm while painting leaves. Store in sealed container in the refrigerator and re-heat to use. Holly berries can also be dipped in shine for an extra glossy look.

C   Alternately, paint on egg white. Use two coats, allowing the first to dry before applying the second. This method is not as long lasting as the gum arabic or gelatine, and produces more a waxy look, rather than shine. It is suitable for flowers that have a waxy look

Lace